Food Safety & Hygiene
Course Book

OTHER PUBLICATIONS IN THE SERIES:

Nutrition in Care (01NC)

Fire Safety (03FS)

Safeguarding Vulnerable Adults (04SV)

End of Life Care, Death and Bereavement (05DB)

Person-Centred Planning (06PC)

Diabetes (07DD)

Stroke (08SS)

Dementia Care (09DC)

Managing Aggression (10MA)

Mental Health Issues (11MH)

Health and Safety (12HS)

Medication (13MM)

Infection Control (14IC)

Equality and Inclusion (15EI)

Mental Capacity and Rights (16MC)

For information on this or other courses please contact:

LEARN CARE EXCEL

Matthews House
21 Thorley Park Road
Bishops Stortford
CM23 3NG

Tel: 07774 880880

info@learncareexcel.co.uk
www.learncareexcel.co.uk

Contents

INTRODUCTION

Even if it's only a small part of their role, it's important that all care staff have a good understanding of safety and hygiene issues when it comes to food preparation. This is because people in care may be vulnerable, are likely to be highly dependent, and could be suffering from various forms of illness. This means that they are relying on the people looking after them to follow the correct procedures when handling food to ensure they do not become seriously ill.

The aim of this course is to cover the laws and legislations around food safety as well as showing how to safely handle food, from ordering and purchase, through storage and preparation right up to consumption and disposal.

As with all the texts in this series, information in this course book is aimed at workers in the care industry and discussion will concentrate particularly on adults in these settings. If you are supporting younger people or people with specific needs please consult further texts.

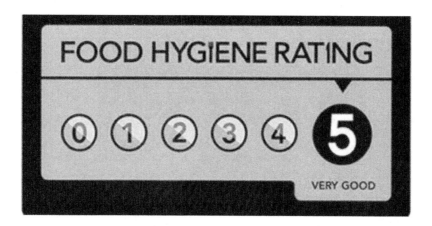

FOOD HAZARDS

The Food Standards Agency describes a hazard as *"something that could be dangerous. And there are lots of different hazards. When we are talking about hazards in relation to food, a hazard is something that could mean that food will not be safe to eat."*

Food Safety hazards can be:

- Biological - involving harmful bacteria, e.g. when certain foods are kept out of the fridge for too long and bacteria grows on them.
- Chemical - involving chemicals getting into food, e.g. cleaning products or pest control chemicals.
- Physical - involving objects getting into food, e.g. broken glass or pieces of packaging

REMEMBER!
These hazards can occur at any time and at any stage. Food safety begins 'the moment you take responsibility for an item'.

FOOD SPOILING AND FOOD-POISONING

There are a number of ways that food can be spoiled including:

FOOD POISONING BACTERIA

Bacteria are only visible when examined under a microscope. Most are not harmful.

Food with food poisoning bacteria may look, smell and taste normal but could make someone ill if it's eaten.   Bacteria that is undesirable in food falls into two categories:

- **Spoilage bacteria**: bacteria that causes food to rot and decay, but does not necessarily make people ill. Meat may develop an odour and fruit may get slimy and these are an indication that food is no longer fit to eat.
- **Pathogens**: a few types of bacteria in food that are responsible for causing illness. They may be present in food in large numbers but are not visible and may not cause obvious changes to the food so that it still looks tastes and smells ok.

Conditions for Bacteria Growth

Bacteria require the following conditions to grow and multiply:

FOOD - Pathogens like to multiply on nutritious foods. These include meat, poultry, fish (particularly shellfish), cooked rice and pasta, milk products and eggs and also any foods that contain these as an ingredient e.g. meat pies, sandwiches, gravy, and salads. Pathogens grow on raw and cooked foods and many raw foods, particularly meat and poultry, contain pathogens. The cooking process kills off pathogens and makes food safe to eat.

MOISTURE - Most foods naturally contain the moisture bacteria need to grow. Bacteria doesn't grow on dehydrated foods such as milk powder, soup mixes.

WARMTH /TEMPERATURE - Pathogens like warmth and will grow at temperatures between 5°C and 63°C, which is often called the 'danger' zone. The optimum temperature for growth is about 37°C. At 37°C (human body temperature) pathogens multiply quickly. But as the temperature continues to rise, their rate slows down and they will stop growing altogether above 63°C. To destroy bacteria, it's recommended that food is cooked at a temperature of 70°C for two minutes.

TIME - In ideal conditions (i.e. in moist foods at 37°C) bacteria grows and multiplies by dividing into two every 20 minutes. After six hours, in ideal conditions, one bacterium cell could multiply to become 131,072 bacteria.

ACIDITY/ALKALINITY - Most bacteria like neutral conditions (pH value of 7) and will not grow in foods with a pH below 4.5. But if pathogens are introduced into an acidic food, they may not necessarily die immediately and could still cause illness.

OXYGEN - Pathogens which require oxygen are known as aerobes, e.g. *Bacillus Cereus*. Some pathogens which don't need oxygen are called anaerobes, e.g. *Clostridium Perfringens and Clostridium* Botulinum. Those that grow or survive with or without oxygen are known as facultative anaerobes and include *Salmonella and Staphylococcus Aureus.*

At the end of this text are details on some common food-poisoning bacteria and their effects.

SPORES

Spores have the constituents of bacteria but don't cause illness and are unable to multiply. Certain bacteria, such as *Bacillus* and *Clostridium*, are able to form spores that are capable of surviving in conditions which active bacteria find unacceptable, e.g. high temperatures or lack of moisture. It means as soon as favourable conditions return the bacteria will grow again.

TOXINS

Some bacteria release poisons known as toxins, which cause food-poisoning. Bacteria such as *Staphylococcus Aureus, Clostridium Botulinum* and *Bacillus Cereus* produce toxins, known as exotoxins, whilst they multiply in food. They're not easily destroyed by cooking and may remain in food once they have developed.

Other bacteria such as *Clostridium perfringens* produce toxins inside the human body only after the food has been eaten. These are referred to as endotoxins.

VIRUSES

Viruses are even smaller than bacteria and can only be seen through an electron microscope. Viral food-poisoning can be caused by the contamination of food by infected food handlers, either from faeces or vomit. If the food is cooked these viruses are destroyed, but contaminated ready-to-eat foods or undercooked foods can cause illness.

Eating shellfish is commonly associated with viral food-poisoning. This is because shellfish are filter feeders and if they feed in water contaminated by sewage they can concentrate the viruses within their bodies. When shellfish are often eaten raw or lightly cooked, illness can occur.

MOULDS

Moulds are a type of fungi that grow on most foods and over a wide range of temperatures. Undesirable moulds tend to lead to food spoilage rather than food-poisoning.

YEASTS

Yeasts are another type of fungi that grows on food. They're used in the manufacture of foods such as bread and beer but also cause spoilage in many foods including jam, fruit juice, yoghurts and meats

CONTROL AND PREVENTION OF FOOD HAZARDS, FOOD SPOILAGE AND FOOD-POISONING

HACCAP (Hazard Analysis Critical Control Points)

The *Food Safety (General Food Hygiene) Regulations* 1995 introduced a requirement for food businesses to take pro-active, preventative measures to make sure the food they produce is safe. A business must be able to demonstrate that they have taken steps to assess a hazard and that 'adequate safety measures are identified, implemented, maintained and reviewed'.

HACCP: The 7 Principles

Principle 1	• Conduct a Hazard Analysis
Principle 2	• Identify the Critical Control Points
Principle 3	• Establish Critical Limits
Principle 4	• Monitor CCP
Principle 5	• Establish Corrective Action
Principle 6	• Verification
Principle 7	• Record Keeping

Think of HACCP as a risk assessment for food. Anyone handling food needs to prevent mistakes which could lead to food poisoning and this involves recognising hazards and putting controls in place.

Below is an example of a HACCP Chart and how it is completed. Note that there may be several hazards and several solutions for evey food situation.

<table>
<tr><td colspan="8" align="center">The Haccp Control Chart</td></tr>
<tr>
<td>Process step</td>
<td>Hazard</td>
<td>Preventative Measure</td>
<td>Critical Limits</td>
<td colspan="2">Monitoring</td>
<td>Corrective Action</td>
<td>Responsibility</td>
</tr>
<tr>
<td></td><td></td><td></td><td></td>
<td>Procedure</td><td>frequency</td>
<td></td><td></td>
</tr>
<tr><td colspan="8">Cooking</td></tr>
<tr>
<td>Cooking</td>
<td>Bacteria survival</td>
<td>Don't under cook food</td>
<td>> 75°C</td>
<td>By knowing that it's cooked</td>
<td>Every time</td>
<td></td>
<td></td>
</tr>
<tr>
<td></td><td></td><td></td><td></td>
<td>Checking temperature with a probe</td>
<td>If your not sure or its hard to tell</td>
<td>Do not remove until the target temperature is reached</td>
<td>Person cooking
Head chef
Sous chef</td>
</tr>
<tr>
<td></td><td></td><td></td><td></td>
<td>If cooking meat then check that the juices run clear</td>
<td>Every time</td>
<td></td><td></td>
</tr>
<tr>
<td></td><td></td><td></td><td></td><td></td><td></td><td></td><td></td>
</tr>
</table>

Food safety procedures

Food safety procedures based on the principles of HACCP are a legal requirement that require:

- Food safety procedures to be permanently kept in place
- Up to date documents and records relating to procedures to be kept
- Procedures to be reviewed if there are changes made to what is produced or how the work is carried out

This process looks at how food is handled and introduces procedures to control hazards. It involves:

- Looking closely at what is done and what could go wrong
- Identifying the 'critical control points': these are the places requiring attention to prevent hazards or reduce them to an acceptable level
- Putting in place procedures to make sure hazards are controlled at critical control points
- Deciding what action to take if something goes wrong
- Making sure that procedures are working
- Keeping appropriate records to show procedures are working

This table demonstrates the possible path food may take from purchase to consumption. Each box and arrow represents a possible control point where a hazard may exist.

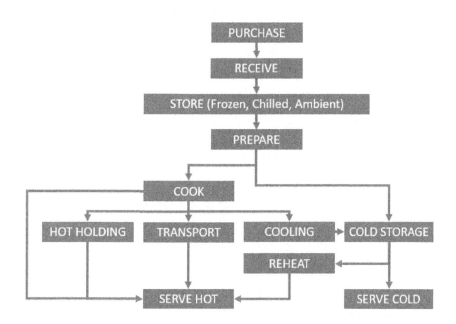

- Prepare food as near to it being eaten as possible and keep it in a fridge until it's ready to eat. DON'T prepare food too far in advance and store at room temperature.

- Cool food quickly and use shallow trays for cooking rice etc. DON'T cool food too slowly and for too long before refrigerating it, especially large joints of meat, turkeys and bulky items cooked in advance.

- Cook to 75°C for 30 seconds. DON'T undercook food.

- Reheat food to 75°C for 30 seconds. DON'T reheat foods on a low temperature.

- Check your supplier takes as much care as you do. DON'T use cooked foods contaminated with food poisoning bacteria.

- Separate raw food from cooked, and use different utensils, sanitise surfaces and keep food covered. AVOID cross contamination from raw food or ready-to-eat food in the kitchen during preparation or in the fridge during storage.

- Thaw in the bottom of the fridge for the time recommended on the label. DON'T inadequately thaw frozen food before cooking, especially poultry.

- Remember the 'danger zone' for bacterial growth is between 5°C and 63°C. DON'T keep food to be sold 'warm' below 63°C and allow bacteria to grow.

- Ensure staff know what to do if they have gastrointestinal illness. DON'T let infected food handlers contaminate food.

- Always cook eggs well. TAKE CARE if eggs only need light cooking e.g. omelettes, mayonnaise.

Examples of hazards and control measures – Fresh chicken fillets

ACTION	WHAT ARE THE DANGERS?	HOW CAN I STOP THEM?
Purchase	· Presence of bacteria on raw foods	· Use a reputable supplier · Check the 'use by' dates
Storage	· Bacteria present on wrapping · Bacteria growth if fridge is not at right temperature · Cross contamination from raw chicken on to ready-to-eat foods already in fridge	· wipe over wrapping if it looks unclean · fridge temp legally needs to be kept at 8°C but preferably 5°C · Store raw foods at bottom of fridge, covered and wrapped
Preparation	· Cross contamination of bacteria onto chicken · Cross contamination from chicken to other foods / surfaces · Presence of bacteria remaining in chicken if not cooked properly	· Wash hands before preparation · Wash work surfaces before preparation · Wear an apron to cover clothing · Use correct chopping boards and knives. · Do not start to prepare food too early, avoid having raw food laying around out of the fridge · Wash all equipment thoroughly after preparation · Wash hands after handling raw chicken · Cook until piping hot throughout. · Use a temperature probe. Chicken should be cooked to a legal minimum of 63°C preferably 75°C to kill salmonella
Service	· Bacteria growing in cooked dishes · Poor handling of leftover food · eating leftovers	· Serve food immediately · If hot holding, food to be kept for no more than two hours below 63°C (only once) after which time, throw it away or chill. · Chill leftovers as quickly as possible. Label them correctly if putting them in fridge · Reheat all foods to a minimum of 75°C. Only ever do this once

Good food hygiene is all about controlling the harmful bacteria that can cause serious illness. When it comes to food hygiene remember the 4 Cs:

- Cross Contamination
- Cleaning
- Chilling
- Cooking

SECTION 1: Cross Contamination

Contamination is the presence of unwanted material, usually microorganisms, in food, which make it unsafe or unpleasant to eat.

Cross-contamination describes the transfer of pathogens from a contaminated food (usually raw items such as meat, poultry and vegetables) to other foods, either directly or indirectly.

Direct Contamination

Contaminating food through touch.
Example: when someone touches a sandwich with dirty hands; when raw meat is placed on top of cooked ham; when a fly lands on food; or when a pet eats from a plate.

Indirect Contamination

The transfer of pathogens on to something that later comes into contact with food.
Example: when someone touches a plate with dirty hands that is later used for sandwiches; when raw meat juices are left on a knife that's then used for slicing ham; when a fly lands on a work surface where food is prepared.

Cross contamination is one of the most common causes of food poisoning, but there are things you can do to minimise the risks.

Avoid food contamination by pathogens. So keep the source of pathogens away from foods, surfaces or utensils.

The sources of pathogens include people, raw foods, pests, pets, air, dust, dirt and food waste. Great care must be taken to stop any pathogens being transferred to foods.

AVOIDING CROSS–CONTAMINATION

To avoid cross-contamination, nothing dangerous should come into contact with food. It is important that high levels of personal hygiene are maintained, including thorough hand washing.

HAND WASHING

Effective hand washing is extremely important to help prevent harmful bacteria from spreading.

REMEMBER!
When it comes to hand washing – take your time!

This hand washing with soap should be carried out frequently, but especially on these occasions:

- Before touching the eyes, nose and mouth
- When entering the food handling area
- After a break or using the toilet
- Before eating or preparing food
- After touching raw food, such as meat/poultry and eggs
- After handling food waste or emptying a bin
- After cleaning
- When hands are contaminated by respiratory secretions, such as coughing or sneezing
- After touching public installations or equipment, such as escalator handrails or doorknobs
- After changing nappies, sanitation items or looking after children or cleaning up vomit
- Before and after visiting hospitals, residential care homes or people who are ill
- After coming into contact with animals or their droppings
- When visibly dirty

Dry hands well and use a disposable paper towel, as cotton towels harbour bacteria.

PERSONAL HYGIENE

REMEMBER!
When it comes to personal hygiene, there are legal requirements to be followed. A simple rinse of the hands and drying them on your clothing isn't enough.

Food handlers should follow these key points:

- Keep long hair tied back and wear a suitable head covering e.g. hat or hairnet, when preparing food. Hair and the scalp carry bacteria, including *Staphylococcus*. Wearing a hat will prevent *physical cross contamination*
- Avoid wearing watches or jewellery other than a plain wedding band
- Don't touch your face and hair, or smoke, spit, sneeze, or eat or chew gum. Half of the population carries *Staphylococcus* pathogens in the nose, mouth and ears. Avoiding this will prevent *microbiological cross contamination*.
- Keep fingernails short and clean, and remove nail polish
- Avoid strong smelling perfumes or aftershaves

CLOTHING AND PROTECTIVE CLOTHING

As clothes pick up pathogens throughout the day and they can easily be the cause of cross-contamination. Carers wear their own clothes but will need to cover up when necessary. This could be a tabards, apron, or plastic disposable apron. If appropriate these items must be laundered separately, preferably on a boil wash.

Footwear must also be appropriate and have low heels, be enclosed, non-slip and clean. Health and safety regulations can also be followed in this area. Advice can be sought from your local authority or the Food Standards Agency.

FITNESS FOR WORK

You must not enter the food handling area if you:
- Are suffering from, or carrying a disease likely to be transmitted through food e.g. the *Campylobacter virus*.
- Have infected wounds/sores /skin infections. High levels of bacteria, such as *Staphylococcus*, can surround open sores. It may be possible, depending on the size and place of the sore, to cover it with a detectable blue plaster.
- Have diarrhoea. Current Department of Health advice is that food handlers suffering from diarrhoea and/or vomiting must be excluded from food handling until they have been symptom free for at least 48hrs.

REMEMBER!
Clean and clear as you go!

This is the most effective form of cleaning and should be used at all times. It means clearing up as you go along, so no bacteria is left hanging around. The clean and clear as you go method applies to all surfaces (floor, worktops, and walls) as well as equipment (knives, boards and cloths).

HIGH PRIORITY CLEANING

High priority cleaning should be carried out for areas that are touched regularly. Handles, taps, switches and can openers should be washed and disinfected often.

FRIDGE CLEANING

The fridge should be cleaned regularly. It's best to do it when it's least full so items don't get too warm when being transferred to another fridge.

WHICH CLEANING CHEMICALS TO USE

This will depend on the individual business and what needs cleaning. But always follow the manufacturer's guidelines when handling cleaning chemicals.

They have been worked out specifically for that product to perform well. Some may need diluting; others can be used neat. Some only work with warm water whereas others will work with cold water. Some chemicals, once diluted, only have a short shelf life. So they need to be clearly dated too.

If pouring a cleaning substance from a large container into a smaller one, always label it clearly. Otherwise chemicals can end up on food inadvertently.

HOW TO CLEAN

- Clear off any obvious debris
- Wash with warm soapy water; this will remove any layers of grease (disinfectant does not cut through grease and bacteria can be stored underneath it)
- Disinfect with a food safe sanitizer or boiling water
- Leave to air dry or use disposable paper towels
- These rules also apply to washing crockery, cutlery and equipment. Ideally, use a dishwasher. If not follow these steps:

    1. Rinse away obvious debris and leftovers
    2. Wash in hot soapy water
    3. Immerse in hot clean water
    4. Leave to air dry, or dry with a disposable cloth
    5. Change the water when it looks dirty

This is known as 'the twin sink method'. The water in the sinks should be very hot; too hot to put your hands in.

MANAGING CLEANING CLOTHS

Your work surfaces, chopping boards and equipment all need washing carefully before preparing food. You should aim to use single cloths wherever possible so that any bacteria collected on them are disposed of straight away.

If you're using reusable cloths, they need to be used carefully. The same cloth shouldn't do two different tasks e.g. wiping cutlery with a cloth that was near raw meat.
Colour coded cloths are a good option.

Reusable cloths should be washed on a high temperature setting in a washing machine separate from other laundry. If you're washing cloths by hand, remove all food debris prior to disinfecting. Cloths should be changed regularly, not just when they look dirty.

REMEMBER!
We cannot see bacteria and appearances can be deceptive. Areas that look clean can still be the perfect breeding ground for bacteria.

Example of a cleaning schedule:

ITEM TO CLEAN	PRODUCT	METHOD OF USE (always follow manufacturers guidelines)	PROTECTIVE CLOTHING	FREQUENCY	CLEANED BY
Floors	Heavy duty cleaner	Using degreaser - prepare a hot solution (half cup full per bucket of water – 2 oz/gal) using a clean mop cover approx 10 – 12 sq.ft. Allow a few moments for solution to act before mopping over with clean fresh water	Wear rubber gloves and suitable footwear	Daily	Alan
Deep fat fryers	Heavy duty degreaser	Drain off fat when cold. Fill with water then add degreaser (1 cupful per bucket of water 4oz/gal) boil up to 20 mins. Brush surrounds with solution. Empty, rinse with clean fresh water. Leave to air dry	Wear rubber gloves and plastic apron	Every 7 days	Mary
Food prep and chopping boards	Cleaning and sanitizing powder	Use powder – fill shaker with powder, then sprinkle on to a moistened surface and scrub. Leave for a few moments for the powder to act. Wipe the surface with a clean moist cloth and allow to air dry	Wear rubber gloves and plastic apron	After each use	All staff

EFFECTIVE PEST CONTROL

Effective pest control is vital to prevent cross contamination. Below is a list of different types of pests and how to control them.

	Evidence	Control
Rats and Mice	Small footprints in dust; Droppings; holes in walls and doors; nests; gnawed goods or packaging; urine stains on packaging	Have a service contract with a pest control agency. Store food off of the floor. Fill any holes. Clean up mess in the kitchen. Keep your refuse area clean and suitably equipped e.g. bins with lids
Flies and flying insects e.g. moths	Bodies of insects; live insects; webbing; nests; droning or buzzing; maggots	Fly-screens at windows and open doors. Electrical bug zappers. Clean kitchen and refuse area. Cover food up
Cockroaches	Eggs and egg cases; moulted 'skins'; live insects; droppings	Don't store food on the floor. Tidy storage and refuse areas. Service contract with pest control agency
Ants	Small piles of sand or soil; live insects; flying ants on hot days	Keep kitchen clean so no spillages anywhere. Care should be taken when using ant powders etc. They should not come into contact with food
Birds	Feathers; droppings; nests; noise; birds	Find out where they are getting in and block it up. Clean up so they have no reason to come in for feeding
Beetles and Weevils	Moving insects, particularly in dry food e.g. flour; small maggots	Store dry foods properly. They should be covered up in between use. Adopt an effective stock rotation system. Always throw suspicious looking goods away

Refuse Storage

Rubbish is a source of contamination, so it should never be allowed to accumulate in a food area.

- Refuse bins should be of minimal size and emptied regularly
- All refuse bins in food rooms should be washable
- Foot operated pedal bins should be used.
- The external refuse store should ideally have a concrete floor
- All rubbish bins should be regularly cleaned to avoid smells

There are legal obligations regarding waste management. More information can be found from the Food Standards Agency or environmental health officer.

Maintenance

Maintenance is critical. If the premises, equipment and utensils are not maintained it can lead to:

- Pests entering through holes in the walls and defective drains
- Cleaning becoming more difficult which may result in a build-up of food debris
- Crockery, cutlery and containers becoming badly worn, broken or unable to be effectively washed and disinfected
- Cracked or broken utensils being a risk of physical contamination
- Physical contamination of food, if equipment, fixtures and fittings are poorly maintained
- Inadequate temperature control in fridges, freezers and cooking equipment could result in food not cooking or freezing to the right temperature

It's a good idea to have contracted service agreements so that any faulty white goods and equipment can be sorted out as soon as possible.

You can also contact the Food Standards Agency for the legal requirements regarding premises structure, and the equipment/utensils that must be supplied.

REFRIGERATING FOOD SAFELY

Some foods need to be kept in a fridge to help stop the growth of bacteria including foods with a 'use by' date, cooked foods and ready-to-eat foods such as desserts and cooked meats. To prevent bacteria growing:

- Keep foods labelled 'keep refrigerated' in the fridge. If the food isn't labelled with any storage instructions and it's a type of food that is likely to go off quickly unless kept chilled, put it in the fridge and eat it within two days.
- When preparing food, keep it out of the fridge for the shortest time possible
- If a dish is not going to be eaten straight away, keep it in the fridge until ready to eat
- Leave food in the fridge until people are ready to eat. Do not leave food out of a fridge for more than four hours
- Cool leftovers as quickly as possible (ideally within one to two hours) and store them in the fridge. Eat any leftovers within two days, except for cooked rice which should be eat within one day.
- Do not put warm food in the fridge or freezer. This will raise the overall temperature and cause bacteria to grow on the food already inside.

FRIDGE FREEZER MANAGEMENT

> **REMEMBER!**
> **Fridges should be kept below 8°C.**
> **Freezers should be kept below -18°C**
>
> **Keep a thermometer in the fridge and record its temperature daily.**

20

FREEZER MANAGEMENT

The star rating system will help ensure that the food frozen is kept safe for consumption. The star-rating system for freezers tells you what it can freeze and for how long. The more stars, the colder the freezer and the longer frozen food can be safely stored.

Star Rating	Freezer Temperature	Food Storage
****	-18°C or colder	Can freeze fresh food, and store food for 3 to 12 months
***	-18°C	Stores pre-frozen food for 3 to 12 months
**	-12°C	Stores pre-frozen food for up to a month
*	-6°C	Stores pre-frozen food for up to a week

DEFROSTING FOOD

- Follow safe food handling practices when defrosting foods, as harmful bacteria can quickly grow if food is not defrosted properly.
- Food that's not defrosted fully before cooking, may not reach a high enough temperature in the middle to kill off bacteria. Food should be put in the fridge to defrost as this keeps the food at safe temperature whilst it thaws.
- Foods that are frozen but ready to eat once thawed, e.g. cheesecake, can be safely defrosted at room temperature as they will not be cooked before eating. Do this in the coolest place for the shortest time.
- Frozen food should be put in the freezer as soon as it's received. If freezing ready-to-eat food, this should be done on the day of receipt. Use an effective labelling system and practice good stock rotation.

SAFE PREPARATION

Raw meat contains harmful bacteria that can spread very easily to anything it touches, including other foods, worktops, chopping boards and knives. It's especially important to keep raw meat away from ready-to-eat foods, such as salad, fruit and bread. This is because these foods won't be cooked before eating, so any bacteria that gets on to these foods won't be killed.

- Don't let raw meat touch other foods
- Never prepare ready-to-eat food using a chopping board or knife that has been used to prepare raw meat, unless they have been washed thoroughly first
- Always wash hands thoroughly after touching raw meat and before touching anything else
- Always cover raw meat and store it on the bottom shelf of the fridge where it can't touch or drip on to other foods

WOODEN CHOPPING BOARDS

It's often thought wooden chopping boards are unhygienic. But a properly washed and sanitised wood cube is a hygienic cutting surface.

- Wash using hot soapy water and a sanitising spray. Heavy soil and scuff marks can be removed with a steel scraper
- Don't put in a dishwasher because of the porous nature of wood. Continual submersion in water and drying will cause the wood to warp and split
- Keep in good condition by regularly scraping with a steel scraper and oiling. While there are special wood oils available, any kitchen cooking oil will waterproof the wood without the risk of contaminating food with the smell of pine or linseed.
- Store cutting boards in an upright position, as this allows air to circulate around the board and help drying

PLASTIC CHOPPING BOARDS

Plastic is the most popular material for chopping boards, because it can be put through a dishwasher and is usually cheaper than wood. Having colour coded chopping boards is a good way of reducing the risk of cross-contamination. There are no legal guidelines regarding which colours should be used. But the accepted coding system in the UK is:

- YELLOW – Cooked meats
- RED – Uncooked meats
- WHITE – Bread and dairy products such as cheese
- BLUE – Raw fish
- GREEN – Salad and fruit
- BROWN – Raw vegetables

COOKING

Thorough cooking kills harmful bacteria in food. So it's extremely important to make sure that food is cooked properly.

> **REMEMBER!**
> **Hot foods must be cooked to 63 °C or above. This is a legal requirement.**
> **(The Food Hygiene (ENGLAND) Regulations.)**

- Hot foods can be kept below 63°c for up to two hours. Only do this once. If any food is left after this time, throw it away, reheat it to 63°C or above, or cool it as quickly as possible to 8°C or below

- Do not top up foods that are being kept warm, as old food at the bottom may be left out for longer than the safe limit.

- Always check that food is piping hot all the way through. Have a temperature probe for food and use this regularly

- Food should be cooked above 63°C. This means the 'core' temperature reaches 63°C not just the edges or topping

- Thoroughly cook poultry and pork, rolled joints and products made from minced meat, such as burgers and sausages as bacteria could be in the middle of these products. They should not be served pink or rare and should be piping hot all the way through.

- Whole cuts of meat, such as steaks, joints of lamb and beef, can be served pink or rare as long as they are fully sealed on the outside.

HOW TO CHECK IF FOOD IS COOKED

Using a food temperature to check if food is cooked to above 75°C. Check batteries are working by placing the thermometer in boiling water or freezing water and checking the temperature.

If there's no access to a probe, use the following:

Chicken. Turkey. Other birds.	Check that birds are cooked properly in the thickest part of the leg. The meat should not be pink or red. The juices should not have any pink or red in them.
Pieces of meat in stews	The largest piece of meat in a stew, curry etc. should be piping hot all the way through and should not have any pink or red in it
Burgers, sausages, processed food	Should be piping hot all the way through with no pink or red inside
Combination foods e.g. shepherd's pie, lasagne	Should be piping hot (steaming) in the centre. If cooking in a large dish/batch, check in several places
Liquid dishes, e.g. soups and sauces	Should bubble rapidly when stirring
Meat joints	Check that all of the outside surfaces of whole cuts of meat and whole joints (beef or lamb) are fully cooked
Rolled meat joints	To check a pork joint or rolled meat joint, insert a skewer into the centre until the juices run out. They should be clear with no traces of pink or red in them
Fish	Cut into the centre of the fish, or by the bone if there is one, to check the colour and texture has changed. Whole pieces of fish e.g. tuna steaks, can be served 'rare' as long as they have been fully seared on the outside

SEPARATING FOODS

To protect against cross-contamination, it's important to keep food separate. This should be done at every stage of food delivery, storage, preparation and serving.

DELIVERY

Delivery times should be planned so raw meat/poultry arrives at different times to other goods. Deliveries should be unloaded in a separate area from the kitchen as packaging can be a cause for cross-contamination.

DEFROSTING

Liquid from defrosting foods can contain bacteria so goods should be defrosted in a covered container, away from cooked and ready-to-eat foods.

STORAGE

If separate fridges aren't available, raw food should be stored beneath cooked food on a lower shelf. Ensure cooked and ready-to-eat foods are covered. Always practice good stock rotation: 'first in, first out'.

PREPARATION

Never use the same chopping boards or knives for preparing raw meat/poultry and ready-to-eat food (unless they have been thoroughly washed and disinfected in between). Think about good practice techniques such as preparing foods separately or at different times of the day.

COOKING

If you're adding raw meat products to a grill make sure they do not touch or drip on to the food that's already cooking.

HIGH RISK FOODS

Certain foods need to be kept chilled to keep them safe e.g.

- Food with a 'use by' date
- Food with 'keep refrigerated' on the label
- Cooked food that will not be served immediately
- Ready-to-eat food such as salads and deserts

The following products are classed as 'high risk', so need to be chilled and handled following legal guidelines:

- All raw, uncooked meats and fish
- Dairy products e.g. soft and semi hard cheeses, dairy based desserts, fromage frais, mousse, crème caramels, products containing cream
- Cooked products containing meat, eggs, fish, soft or hard cheeses, cereals (rice and grains) pulses and vegetables
- Smoked or cured ready-to-eat meat or fish, e.g. ham, smoked fish, some salamis
- Prepared ready-to-eat foods e.g. prepared veg, vegetable salads, coleslaw, sandwiches
- Uncooked or partly cooked pastry and dough products, e.g. pizzas or fresh pasta containing meat, fish or veg

KEEP FOOD SAFE

When using equipment including fridges of chill cabinets:

- Follow the manufacturer's instructions
- Pre-cool the unit before putting chilled food in it. It is recommended that fridges and chilled display equipment is set at 5°C or below.
- Only display as much food as needed
- Display food for the shortest time possible

Temperatures

As we know, bacteria that causes food poisoning grow at temperatures between 5°C and 63°C (40°F-145°F). They grow most rapidly at a temperature of 37°C (98°F), which is the normal temperature of the human body.

REMEMBER!
The temperature danger zone is between 5°C and 63°C.
Store high risk foods below 5°C or above 63°C.

FOOD ITEM	METHOD OF STORAGE	USEFUL TIPS
Raw meat, poultry and game.	Refrigerate at temperature below 8°C, preferably hung with drip trays beneath.	Store away from cooked meat and cooked meat products to avoid any risk of cross-contamination.
Raw meat products, sausages, mince, etc.	Refrigerate at temperature below 8°C	As above.
Bacon, whole cured ham.	Refrigerate at temperature below 8°C, if sliced but otherwise may be hung in a cold dry place protected from dirt and insects.	Store away from raw meat and meat products.
Cooked meat & cooked meat products.	Refrigerate at temperature below 8°C.	Store away from raw meat and meat products.
Fish (fresh).	Refrigerate at temperature below 8°C, preferably in separate compartments or in lidded fish trays away from other foods which may become tainted.	
Fish (frozen).	Deep freezer kept at -18°C.	Frozen fish should be thawed only immediately before use.
Fish (smoked or cured).	Keep in chill storage, at A temperature below 8°C, away from other foods which may become tainted.	
Fruit (fresh and dried).	Store in cool, dry, well ventilated place away from other food at least 150mm from the ground.	Discard at the first sign of mould growth. Do not overstock. Wash before serving or cooking.
Flour and cereals.	Store in self-closing tightly lidded containers in dry cool area.	

Fresh eggs.	Refrigerate at temperature below 8°C.	Use strictly in rotation. Safer still use pasteurised eggs.
Fats, butter, margarine.	Refrigerate at temperature below 8°C.	Store away from highly flavoured food which may taint.
Milk (fresh).	Refrigerate below 8°C separately in compartment	Strict rotation should apply Wipe sides and bottom of bottles with clean cloth before refrigerating.
Milk (powders).	Cool well ventilated dry place in original container.	Reconstitute only immediately before use.
Prepared sweets, jellies, trifles, custards, etc., creams, synthetic fillings, and casings (pastry, etc) containing these.	Refrigerate at temperature below 8°C if prepared more than 4 hours in advance.	Should be prepared only on day of use.
Gravies, soups, etc.	Refrigerate at temperature below 8°C if prepared more than 4 hours in advance.	Should be prepared only on day of use.
Rice (uncooked) Pasta (dried).	Store in a suitable covered container.	Keep dry.
Rice (cooked) Pasta (fresh).	Cook as near to time of service as possible. If it is to be used in a salad chill quickly and refrigerate at temperature below 8°C.	Do not re-heat rice.
Sugar, salt, bread	In tightly lidded bins in cool, dry place.	
Canned goods (unopened).	Cool, dry, well ventilated place preferably in original cartons.	Blown, rusty or split tins must not be used.
Bottled goods including jams, preserves, etc.	Cool dry well ventilated Place.	Cool dry well ventilated place.
Root vegetables.	May be stored in sacks or nets as delivered in cool, dry ace.	Use leaf vegetables on day of receipt otherwise inspect frequently for deterioration. Root vegetables should not be stored in plastic sacks or sacks which have become damp or wet.
Other vegetables	Store on racks with adequate air circulation. In a cool, dry place.	As above.

UNDERSTANDING CULTURAL DIFFERENCES

This section gives a brief outline on some cultural and religious differences in relation to food.

Hinduism

Most Hindus are vegetarians and do not eat meat or animal by-products including gelatine, which is found in sweets. Those that do eat meat do not eat cows as they're regarded as sacred animals. Vegetarian Hindus see food as being contaminated if it is stored and prepared near meat. Separate cooking utensils and equipment should be used when preparing vegetarian food.

Judaism

Jewish diets have to be kosher (permitted). This means that animals have to be slaughtered by qualified slaughterer. Forbidden foods include, horses, pigs, rabbits, birds of prey and shellfish. Kosher meats are all sources of meat with split hooves and that chew the cud, kosher chicken and their eggs, and kosher fish that have both fins and scales such as cod. Fruit and vegetables are kosher as long as they have not been cooked with non-kosher ingredients. Jewish law prohibits the mixing of milk foods with meat foods. Fish can be served with milk, and also be served with meat dishes. Separate utensils and serving tools should be used for both items, with a period of time observed between eating the two items.

Islam

Muslims do not eat pork or any pig products; they will only eat Halal meat that is killed by Islamic laws. Dairy products are acceptable if Halal. Fish and vegetables are permitted. Foods containing animal by-products are not permitted. No alcohol is permitted.

Rastafarianism

Most are vegetarians, and avoid meat, fish and poultry. Others are vegans and will not eat and animal by-products including fat, milk or gelatine. Some choose to eat meat, but will not eat pork, as it is seen as unclean meat.

Sikhism

Meat should only be consumed if it is Jhatka, where the animal has been instantaneously killed with one stroke. Sikhs will not eat halal or kosher meat. Many Sikhs are vegetarians.

Jainism

Most Jains do not like to hurt other animals so are vegetarian. Storage and preparation is important too. Some Jains avoid root crops such as carrots.

Christianity

Christians have no specific dietary requirements but will often choose fish on Fridays to honour Christ's death.

The Environmental Health Officer

The environmental health officer deals with a wide range of issues, including:
- Food safety
- Environmental protection and pollution control
- Noise control
- Health and safety at work
- Public health
- Waste management

Their duties involve all aspects of inspecting businesses for health and safety, food hygiene and food standards including:
- Collecting samples for laboratory testing
- Enforcing environmental health laws
- Investigating accidents at work
- Advising community groups and giving educational talks
- Giving evidence in cases that come to court
- Keeping records and writing reports
- Following up complaints
- Investigating outbreaks of food poisoning, infectious disease or pests

The Food Standards Agency

The *Food Standards Act* 1999 led to the formation of a Food Standards Agency, which protects consumer interests in regards to food safety and standards. The agency lets the public know what advice it gives to government, and act openly and independently when it comes to looking after the interests of consumers.

In *Food Hygiene, a Guide for Businesses*, published by the agency, the most important food hygiene regulations for businesses are:
- Regulation (EC) No. 852/2004 on the hygiene of foodstuffs
- The Food Safety and Hygiene (England) Regulations 2013 (These regulations revoked The Food Hygiene (England) Regulations 2006.)

These regulations set out the basic hygiene requirements for all aspects of business, from premises and facilities to the personal hygiene of staff. It's essential for all businesses to show what steps it has taken to make or sell food that is safe to eat, and ensure this information is recorded.

The Food Safety Act 1990

Under the *Food Safety Act* 1990 a business:

- Must not sell (or keep for sale) food that is 'unfit' for people to eat
- Must not cause food to be dangerous to health
- Must not sell food that is not what the customer is entitled to expect, in terms of quality or quantity
- Must not describe food in a way that is false or misleading

Food is deemed to be unsafe if it is considered to be:

- Injurious to health
- Unfit for human consumption

The Food Safety and Hygiene (ENGLAND) Regulations 2013

This regulation makes it easier for businesses to find food safety and food hygiene legal requirements that are relevant to them. It states that:

- The walls, floors, ceilings, doors, windows and food contact surfaces in all food premises must be maintained in good repair and condition to permit adequate cleaning/disinfection with no danger of contamination by external sources such as pests.
- Drainage facilities must be adequate and they must be designed and constructed to avoid the risk of contamination of foodstuffs.
- An effective cleaning schedule should be implemented to cover all of the premises and all the equipment in it. The type of material used that is suitable for surfaces will depend upon the activity in each room. It's recommended that areas which are subject to intense use are finished to provide a more durable surface.

REMEMBER!
If poor food hygiene practices result in prosecution the individual responsible can be identified and prosecuted and fined.

Salmonella

Salmonella food-poisoning may cause serious illness, even fatalities in vulnerable people e.g. older people, babies and those who are already ill.

It's found in the guts of animals, including farm animals and especially poultry and the bacteria is transferred to the meat during the slaughtering process. It's also found in or on eggs, in unpasteurised milk, rats, mice, and domestic pets, including terrapins.

People may also be a source, particularly after suffering from symptoms of Salmonella food poisoning, which may continue to excrete from them for a long period after recovery.

Salmonella bacteria cause illness by multiplying within the human body and causing an infection.

Symptoms: fever, vomiting, abdominal pains and diarrhoea, (septicaemia or peritonitis may occasionally develop)

Onset: 6 - 72 hours, but usually 12 – 36 hours.

Duration: 1 - 8 days, but can be longer.

Control Measures:
- Avoid use of raw eggs in foods such as mayonnaise, uncooked desserts. Catering outlets can obtain pasteurised eggs
- Keep raw meats and poultry away from other foods to prevent cross- contamination
- Keep foods at correct temperatures
- Keep animals away from foods
- Practise good personal hygiene

Bacteria are hitchhikers.

E. Coli

There are several types of *E.coli*. Not all are harmful, but certain strains are pathogenic, usually causing symptoms of diarrhoea. One type, *E. coli O157*, causes serious illness and even death, particularly in young children and older people.

E. coli O157 is found in the gut of farm animals. People get ill after eating undercooked meat and unpasteurised dairy products and by having contact with farm animals.

Since low numbers of these bacteria can cause illness, avoiding cross-contamination from raw to cooked or ready-to-eat foods is important. It can be spread via hands, kitchen surfaces and cooking utensils such as chopping boards and knives that can become contaminated when preparing raw meat. If utensils are not properly washed, they can transfer bacteria on to other foods, which can cause food poisoning.

It can also spread from person to person, both in families and in institutions such as schools and residential homes.

Symptoms: watery and sometimes bloody diarrhoea, severe abdominal cramps, and occasionally kidney damage (in more serious cases).

Onset: usually 3 - 4 days, but ranges from 1 - 14 days.

Duration: usually two weeks but longer if complications, such as kidney damage develop.

Controls:
- Prevent this infection by handling and cooking meat in a safe way.
- Wash hands carefully with soap before starting to cook
- Cook ground beef until no pink meat can be seen anywhere
- Don't taste small bites of raw ground beef while you're cooking
- Don't put cooked hamburgers on a plate that had raw ground beef on it before
- Defrost meats in the fridge or microwave. Don't let meat sit on the counter to defrost
- Keep raw meat and poultry separate from other foods.
- Use hot water and soap to wash cutting boards and dishes if raw meat and poultry have touched them
- Keep food refrigerated or frozen
- Keep hot food hot and cold food cold
- Refrigerate leftovers right away or throw them away
- People with diarrhoea should wash their hands carefully and often, using hot water and soap, and washing for at least 30 seconds
- People working in day care centres and homes for the elderly should frequently wash their hands

Staphylococci Aureus

Most outbreaks are caused by food being contaminated with bacteria from the nose, throat or skin lesions. *Staphylococci* produce toxins whilst growing in food, so when the food is eaten the toxins cause vomiting.

Staphylococci produce toxins in food that are resistant to heat so won't be destroyed during the cooking process

Symptoms: vomiting, stomach pains, diarrhoea.

Onset: 1 - 7 hours.

Duration: 6 - 24 hours

Controls:

Vomiting

- Practise good personal hygiene
- Pay attention to hand washing before food preparation involving direct handling of foods.
- Cover cuts
- Avoid sneezing, coughing, etc.
- Refrigerate foods rich in nutrients, particularly those that have been handled
- Prevent food handlers contaminating food
- Avoid handling food where possible
- Don't eat or smoke in food rooms
- Ensure hot food is stored above 63ºC

Bacillus Cereus

Bacillus Cereus produces a toxin in food that appears as the bacteria forms spores. The toxin is not easily destroyed by normal cooking.

Food-poisoning cases mostly occur when rice and pasta dishes have not been kept at the correct temperatures.

Symptoms: vomiting, stomach cramps and some diarrhoea.

Onset: 1 - 5 hours.

Duration: usually no longer than 24 - 36 hours.

Controls:

- Always cook food thoroughly
- Ensure meats are cooked by probing them with a knife. If the juices run clear then the meat can be eaten. If there is any blood the meat requires cooking for longer
- Prevent cross-contamination by keeping cooked and raw food separate
- Store ready-to-eat cooked foods at the top and raw foods at the bottom of the fridge
- Any work surfaces, equipment and utensils used to handle raw meat should be cleaned before it is used to handle cooked meats
- Allow all frozen foods, especially frozen poultry and large joints of meat, to thaw out completely in a fridge before cooking them
- Cooked food must not be left out longer than two hours. After this period food should be placed in the fridge, even if it is still warm. Large dishes may need to be split into a number of smaller receptacles to help them cool down quicker
- Food items kept in the fridge should be stored at a temperature lower than 8°C.
- On hot summer days the fridge should be checked to ensure it is operating at the correct temperature
- Keep pets away from food and food preparation area. Always wash hands after handling pets
- Wash hands thoroughly after using the toilet and ensure that children wash their hands

Campylobacter

These bacteria are the most common cause of diarrhoea in the UK with most cases being caused by the type *C. jejuni*.

Campylobacter do not grow in food. Illness can be caused if the food is contaminated by small numbers of the pathogen. It has also been related to drinking water and to coming into contact with animals.

Symptoms: very severe abdominal pain, diarrhoea, headaches and nausea. People are rarely sick. Often confused with appendicitis because of the severe pain and fever.

Onset: 1 - 10 days (usually 2 – 5 days).

Duration: 1 - 7 days. A second dose of illness may sometimes occur about 3 weeks after the first symptoms developed.

Controls:
- Keep animals and birds away from food, including bottled milk
- Wash hands after dealing with pets
- Cook all poultry products thoroughly. Make sure that meat is cooked throughout and any juices run clear
- Cook poultry to reach a minimum internal temperature of 165°F
- Wash hands with soap before preparing food
- Wash hands with soap after handling raw foods of animal origin and before touching anything else
- Prevent cross-contamination in the kitchen by using separate cutting boards for foods of animal origin and other foods and by carefully cleaning all cutting boards, countertops, and utensils with soap and hot water after preparing raw food of animal origin
- Avoid consuming unpasteurised milk and untreated surface water.
- Make sure that persons with diarrhoea, especially children, wash their hands carefully and frequently with soap to reduce the risk of spreading the infection
- Wash hands with soap after contact with pet faeces

Bacteria	A group of microorganisms. Most are harmless; a few cause illness such as food-poisoning
Best before date	Date given by manufacturer to indicate when food should be eaten by in order to be in its best condition
Contamination	The presence of microorganisms in food which may make it unsafe to eat
Cross-Contamination	Transfer of pathogens from contaminated food (usually raw) to other foods
Danger Zone	The temperature range in which pathogens will multiply i.e. 5° to 63°C
Food Poisoning	An illness caused by eating contaminated food
Food Spoilage	The effect of certain types of moulds, yeasts or bacteria which cause food to go off or rot
Hazard	Something which has the potential to lead to food-poisoning e.g. the presence of pathogens on raw meat
Hazard Control	Action by which a hazard can be prevented e.g. cooking food to kill any pathogens
High Risk Foods	Foods in which pathogens can easily multiply; these are usually moist and rich in nutrients
Microorganisms	Very small living organisms including bacteria, viruses, moulds and yeasts
Pathogens	Microorganisms which cause illnesses such as food-poisoning
Personal hygiene	Practices which should be followed to make sure personal habits do not make food unsafe to eat
Preserving food	Using methods to stop or slow down the multiplication of microorganisms in order to keep foods for longer periods of time
Rules of Food Hygiene	Practices which should be followed to ensure food is safe to eat
Source of Bacteria	Place where bacteria are found
Spores	A form which some bacteria take to protect themselves against conditions which they do not like such as high temperatures
Toxins Poisons	Which are produced by some bacteria, for example, when they multiply in food
Use by Date	Date given by the manufacturer, marked on some perishable foods, by which food must be eaten to ensure that it is safe to eat and it has not gone off

For information on more courses please contact:

LEARN CARE EXCEL
Matthews House
21 Thorley Park Road
Bishops Stortford
CM23 3NG

Tel: 07774 880880

info@learncareexcel.co.uk
www.learncareexcel.co.uk

Printed in Great Britain
by Amazon

42681060R00024

Business Process Modelling with BPMN

Modelling and Designing Business Processes Course Book
using the Business Process Model and Notation
Specification Version 2.0

Kenneth J Sherry

First Published in 2012

By Admaks Training and Publications

www.admaks.com

Copyright © Admaks Training and Publications

BPMN Course Book

The BPMN course book has been specifically designed by Admaks. This is a comprehensive course book covering all parts of the BPMN specification version 2.0. Each BPMN element is explained at length using diagrams and descriptions, including modelling a complete business process. After completing the course book, readers will be able to create clearly defined and organised BPMN diagrams.

Table of Contents

Introduction to BPMN

It is becoming more and more important for the business world to understand what processes are and when modelled, to read and understand them. This is one of the main reasons that the Business Process Modelling Notation was developed, to enable the Business World to understand diagrammatically what business processes look like and what they represent. It resulted in a set of notation categories so that the reader could easily recognise the basic types of elements and understand the diagram. Additional variation and information can be added by the modeller to support the requirements for complexity, within the basic categories of elements, without dramatically changing the basic look-and-feel of the diagram. Using BPMN allows almost any process to be clearly defined and organised with the minimum of confusion, in such a way that virtually anyone can follow the results.

What is a Process

A process is a continuous action, operation or series of changes taking place in a specific manner. A process is made up of tasks, roles and resources. It must have an owner, be an activity and be driven by inputs and outputs. A task can be anything that is performed in daily activities and can be as simple as making breakfast, having a shower or producing customer invoices.

Everyday process

Making dinner is an everyday process and is a series of tasks completed in a specific sequence.

Write out a task list of things you do to make dinner

Task list for making dinner	Your Tasks
1 Find recipe	1
2 Shop or find ingredients	2
3 Prepare ingredients and cook	3
4 Lay table	4
5 Serve and eat meal	5
6 Clear table and wash up	6
	7

Table - Task list of making dinner

The above task list can be shown in the following diagram as a series of tasks

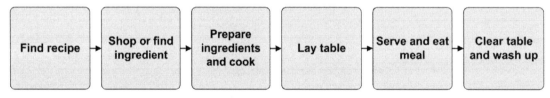

Diagram – Sequence of tasks for making dinner

Modelling Definitions

Process: a sequence of tasks, decisions and events using inputs. A complex process can be broken down into groups of tasks and decisions called a Sub-process.

Sub-process: tasks, decisions and events which are part of an overall process, which contain an aim, an input and an output.

Task: the definitive part of a process that describes an activity, e.g. producing an invoice, making coffee etc.

Decision: a change in the process sequence flow.

Procedure: a sequence of actions or instructions to be followed in order to accomplish a task or solve a problem.

Notation: set of graphical symbols for a specific use which replaces a written description.

Set of basic types of BPMN notations

Task notations are represented by a rounded-corner rectangle.

A task is any type of action or activity which is undertaken and produces a result.

Collapsed sub-process notations are rounded-corner rectangles distinguished by a plus sign in a square, bottom centre of the shape.

A collapsed sub-process notation is used to depict a set of activities or tasks within a process which cannot be seen.

The above are considered a Generic type of *task* or Generic *collapsed sub-process* and are the most commonly used. Their only requirement is to perform the described activity.

Gateway notations are represented by a diamond shape.

Gateway notations are used to control how *sequence flows* interact as they join and fork within a process.

An *event* is an incident that takes place during the course of a business process and is used to control the process sequence. Events are depicted by circles with open centres to allow internal markers to differentiate between triggers or results. There are two types of generic events which affect the process flow, *start* and *end* event.

A process flow requires a *sequence flow* notation to connect the activities, gateways and events. This is depicted by a solid line with a solid arrow head at one end.

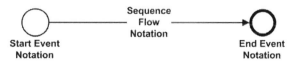

Business Process Diagram (BPD)

BPMN is represented by a diagram based on a flowcharting technique tailored for creating graphical models of business process operations. Diagrams are used because they are intuitive and provide an easy to remember and understandable visualisation of a business process. These diagrams are called Business Process Diagrams (BPD) and are made up of a set of graphical elements which enable the easy development of simple diagrams. The BPMN elements are designed to be distinguishable from each other and to utilise shapes that are familiar.

Making Dinner revisited

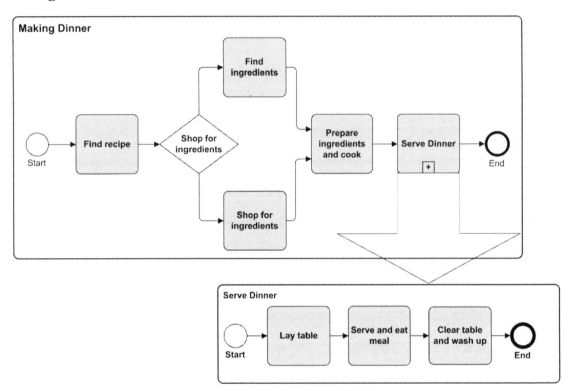

Diagram - Making dinner BPD

The above diagram shows the previous diagram *Sequence of tasks for making dinner* using BPMN elements.

The **Start** and **End** events have been introduced.

A **Decision** gateway to *Shop for Ingredients* was used to branch the process sequence, to either *Shop for Ingredients* or *Find the Ingredients*.

The **Sub-process** called *Serve Dinner* contains three tasks, *Lay table, Serve and eat meal* and the most exciting task of all, *Clear table and wash up*.

The diagram demonstrates the use of a BPD and the techniques used to represent a process and sub-process

---

Question: Is the sub-process Serve Dinner necessary and if not how else could the process be modelled?

Basic Business Process Modelling

When setting out to model a business process, it is recommended to begin with an overall picture of the process and design a high level business processes diagram (BPD). Once the BPD has been designed, then the job of process modelling can begin.

The diagram below illustrates the process of *Going to work* which has been broken into two, sequential sub-processes:

1. *Getting ready for work*
2. *Commuting to work*

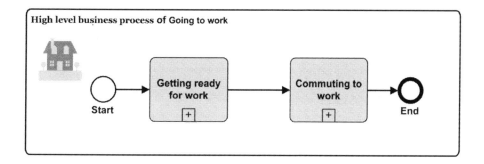

Diagram – High level business process of *Going to work*

The above diagram is a BPD which uses BPMN notations and has a **Start** and an **End** event. As in any process design, all the requirements must be first gathered and then broken down into tasks. These tasks are modelled in a sequential manner to show the flow of each task and where it takes place in the process flow.

Notes

Getting ready for work

The following is a list of tasks to be performed in Getting Ready for Work which also includes decisions to be made during the process sequence flow.

Getting ready for work	
Tasks and decisions involved	**Activity**
Wake up and get out of bed	task
Bathroom or breakfast	decision
Make breakfast	task
Eat breakfast	task
Have a shower	task
Get dressed	task
Dressed and showered	decision
Breakfast	decision
Pick up your bag and keys	task
Close the door and leave	task

Exercise – Getting ready for work

List your tasks and decisions for Getting ready for work	
Tasks and decisions involved	**Activity**

Using the previous task list, the following BPD represents the sub-process of **Getting ready for work**.

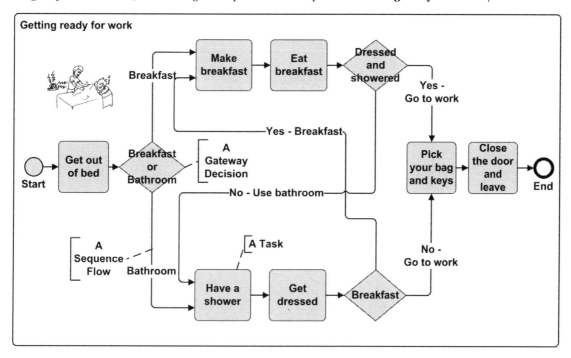

Diagram – Getting ready for work

- The process begins with the **Start** event, activates the *Get out of bed task,* the sequence then flows to a **Decision** gate (Breakfast or Bathroom)
- Further decisions are made depending on the first decision in the sequence (Breakfast or Bathroom)
- The process sequence flows though more tasks and decisions and finishes with the task *Close the door and leave* and an **End** event

Exercise – Sub-process Getting ready for work

From your list of tasks and decisions for Getting Ready for Work, model the process BPD

Process name:

Notes

Commuting to work

The following is a list of tasks to be performed in *Commuting to work,* which also includes decisions to be made during the process sequence flow.

Commuting to work task list	
Tasks and decisions involved	**Activity**
Leave home	task
Take car or bus	decision
Stand and wait for a bus	task
Get on the bus	task
Bus pass or ticket	decision
Buy a ticket find a seat	task
Show pass find a seat	task
Wait for stop	task
Stay on or get off	decision
Walk to exit	task
Press the stop button	task
Bus stops, alight and go to the office	task

Exercise – Task list Commuting to work

List your tasks and decisions for Commuting to work	
Tasks and decisions involved	**Activity**

Using the previous task list, the following BPD represents the sub-process **Commuting to work**

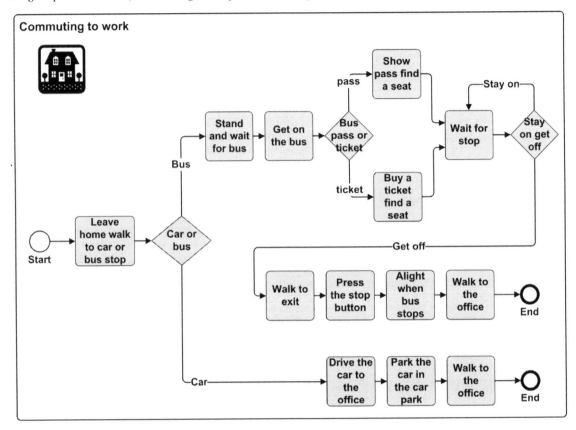

Diagram – Commuting to work

- The Start event activates the *Leave home and walk to car or bus stop* task
- If the **Decision** is to take the car the sequence goes to *Drive the car to the office, Park the car in the car park* and *Walk to the office*, then concludes with an **End** event
- If the **Decision** is to take the bus, the sequence flows to further tasks before reaching the **Decision,** *Bus pass or ticket*
- If a ticket must be purchased, the sequence goes to *Buy a ticket find a seat task*, if not, proceeds to *Show pass find a seat task*
- The process sequence continues until the **Decision,** *Stay on or get off* is reached, then the process task sequence continues through *Walk to exit, Press the stop button, Alight when Bus Stops, Walk to the Office* and finally, the **End** event

Exercise –Sub-process Commuting to work

From your list of tasks and decisions for Commuting to work model the process BDP

Process name:

Start

End

Notes

Task Procedure

A task procedure details the activities within the task and is a sequence of actions or instructions to be followed, to accomplish the task or solve a problem. The procedure of a task will vary, depending on the person, situation, circumstances and timing.

As is shown in BPD *Getting Ready for Work*, each task has a step by step procedure which may be documented depending on the process requirements. The task procedure document could be used by fulfilment staff in a situation which requires a definite procedure to be followed

Example of a Task Procedure

From the sub-process of *Getting ready for work* the following task procedure describes the task of *Have a shower*. The following task procedure outline could be utilised where a step by step procedure is required.

Task procedure for Have a shower		
Procedure number	Procedure steps	Your Procedure steps
1	Enter the bathroom	
2	Start the shower	
3	Adjust to the correct temperature	
4	Remove pyjamas	
5	Get in the shower	
6	Close shower door	
7	Find the shower soap	
8	Lather up	
9	Wash the soap off	
10	Turn off shower	
11	Get out of the shower	
12	Find the towel	
13	Towel dry	
14	Put on dressing gown	
15	Leave the bathroom	

Table – Task procedure

Exercise – Procedure taking a shower

Document **your** procedure steps for *Have a shower*

Exercise - Commuting to work task

From the sub-process *Commuting to work* list the tasks which could be a procedure

-
-
-

BPMN Activity Notations

An activity is defined as work which is performed within a business process. There are two types of notations used, the *task* and the *sub-process*. The *task* is an activity performed at a specific point in the process sequence. The *sub-process* is a container of groups of tasks and can also contain further *sub-processes*. Each *task* or *sub-process* must perform some form of work on incoming information, therefore producing an output.

The *task* and *collapsed sub-process* notations are graphically shown by the same rounded corner rectangular symbol however, the *collapsed sub-process* is differentiated by a plus sign centre bottom.

A *collapsed sub-process* notation is used to depict a set of activities or tasks within a process which are not shown.

There are 5 distinct types of notations

- Unspecified / none
- Looping
- Parallel Multi-Instance
- Sequential Multi- Instance
- Adhoc

Unspecified / None Activity Notations

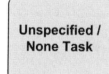 

The *unspecified / none* form of the *task* and *collapsed sub-process* notations, is a rectangle with rounded corners. The *unspecified / none* type of *task* or *collapsed sub-process* is the most common and is used in most circumstances. Its only requirement is to perform the described activity.

Looping Activity Notations

A *looping* notation is shown as a circle with an arrow on the end placed in the centre bottom of the rectangle. The *looping task* or *collapsed looping sub-process* notations are used to show that the same specific *task* or *sub-process* is performed a number of times, before continuing the sequence flow.

Multi-instance Tasks and Sub-processes

The *multi-instance task* or *collapsed sub-process* may be executed in parallel or be sequential. Either an expression is used to specify or calculate the desired number of instances or a data driven setup is used. If data input is specified, the number of items in the data collection determines the number of activity instances. This data input can be produced by an input data association.

Multi-instance Parallel Notations

The *multi-instance parallel* notation has 3 parallel vertical lines in the centre bottom of the element. The *multi-instance parallel task* and *collapsed sub-process* notations describe multiple parallel activities. These are used when 2 or more of the same task or sub-process is performed simultaneously.

Multi-instance Sequential Notations

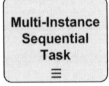 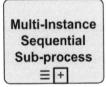

The *multi-instance sequential* notation has 3 parallel horizontal lines in the centre bottom of the element. The *multi-Instance sequential task* and *collapsed sub-process* describes multiple parallel activities. These are used when 2 or more of the same task or sub-process is performed simultaneously.

The characteristic markers (*looping, multi-instance parallel* and m*ulti-instance sequential*) are mutually exclusive markers and only one of them can be depicted on a single activity.

Ad-Hoc Sub-processes Notation

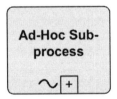

The *Ad-Hoc* notation is represented by a wavy line in the middle of the bottom of the element. The *Ad-Hoc collapsed sub-process* describes a situation that does not have a pre-defined sequence flow. The tasks and sub-processes are not performed in any pre-determined flow and therefore considered Ad-Hoc. The possibility of an *Ad-Hoc sub-process* as a looping sub-process is conceivable but it is not shown here.

Expanded Sub-process

An *expanded sub-process* notation is shown as a separate diagram. The tasks, sub-processes, decisions and events, required to perform the sub-process are depicted inside the expanded sub-process.

If the collapsed sub-process has an activity symbol, this is shown within the expanded sub-process diagram:

There are 5 types of expanded sub-process notations

- None / Unspecified
- Multi-Instance
- Looping
- Compensation
- Ad-Hoc

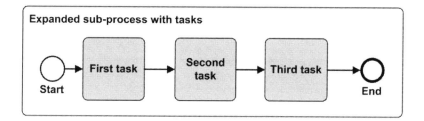

Diagram - Expanded sub-process with tasks

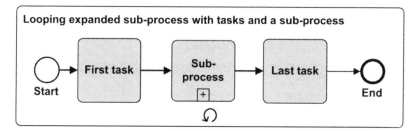

Diagram - Looping expanded sub-process with tasks and a sub-process

Example of a Process using unspecified / none task types

It is necessary to take a vacation from time to time and therefore there are some decisions to be made and tasks to be fulfilled. The following is a list of decisions and tasks needed to organise a vacation.

Tasks

Decide when and where

Use travel agency:

- Select travel agency
- Go to travel to agency
- Book vacation at agency

Self booking:

- Use internet - Yes:

  Search for vacations

- Use Internet - No:
    - Order vacation brochure
    - Receive vacation brochure
- Select vacation and dates
- Book flights and hotels

The following diagram depicts a process of selecting and booking a vacation. This example uses unspecified / none task elements.

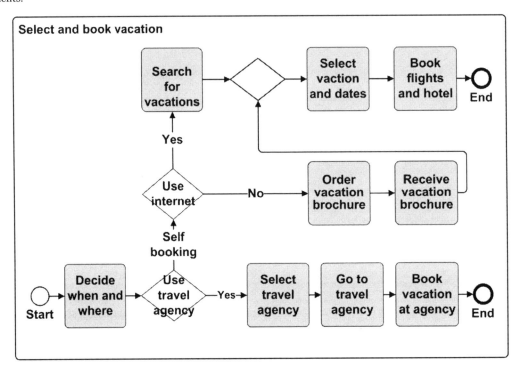

Diagram - Select and book vacation

Send Task Notation

A *send task* notation is shown by a rectangle with rounded corners containing a filled envelope marker in the upper left corner.

The *send task* is used to show that a message is to be sent to an external participant, relative to the process. Once the message has been sent, the task is completed. The actual participant, to whom the message is sent, can be identified by connecting the send task to a *participant,* using a message flow connector.

Receive Task Notation

A *receive task* notation is shown by a rectangle with rounded corners containing an unfilled envelope marker in the upper left corner.

The *receive task* starts a process if the process sequence does not have a start event and the *receive task* has no incoming sequence flow. If the *receive task* has an incoming sequence flow, the task is not used to start the process. If the *receive task* references a message, there can only be one data output. If a data output is referenced, it must be equivalent to the message defined by the incoming associated message. When the *receive task* is used to start a process, the process sequence is controlled by the receipt of a message.

Human Interaction Tasks

Human involvement is required to complete certain tasks specified in a workflow model. BPMN specifies two different types of tasks with human involvement, manual task and user task.

Manual Task Notation

A m*anual task* notation is shown by a rectangle with rounded corners with the addition of a hand figure marker, which distinguishes the shape as a *manual task* type.

The *manual task* is a task that is expected to be performed without the aid of any computer technology.

User Task Notation

A *user task* notation is shown by a rectangle with rounded corners with the addition of a human figure marker, which distinguishes the shape as a *user task* type.

The *user task* is primarily used as a workflow task in which a human performs the task, with or without the assistance of a software application.

Business Rule Task Notation

A *business rule task* notation is shown by a rectangle with rounded corners with the addition of a chart shape in the upper left corner, indicating the task is a *business rule task*.

The *business rule task* provides a mechanism for the process to provide input to a business rules engine and to receive the output of calculations that the business rules engine provides. The input output specification of the task allows the process to send data to and from a business rules engine.

Script Task Notation

A s*cript task* notation is shown by a rectangle with rounded corners with the addition of a script shape in the upper left corner, indicating the task is a s*cript task* type.

The *script task* activity is driven by a software application which executes the script. When the script is executed the task is complete.

Service Task Notation

A *service task* notation is shown by a rectangle with rounded corners with the addition of a set of mechanical cogs in the upper left corner, indicating the task is a *service task* type.

The *Sservice task* links to an external service e.g. web application and has one input and at most one output. The Service Task is linked to a participant's service, using a message flow within a collaboration process.

Exercise – Task types

The previous process diagram *select and book vacation* described a process of booking a vacation using unspecified / none tasks. Using the diagram *select and book vacation* decide which task type should be used for each activity (some tasks types can be used more than once) .

Complete the table below.

Task	Type
Decide when and where	
Select travel agency	
Go to travel to agency	
Book vacation at agency	
Search for vacations	
Order vacation brochure	
Receive vacation brochure	
Select vacation and dates	
Book flights and hotels	

Table – Book a vacation list of tasks

Exercise - Looping task

Using the previous diagram - *select and book vacation* decide which tasks could be modelled as looping tasks.

Write down the task names and the number of times to be performed

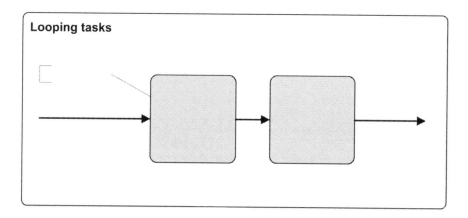

BPMN Gateway Notations

Gateways are modelling notations which are used to control how *sequence flows* interact as they merge, join and fork within a process. A *gateway* can be thought of as a question that is asked at a point in the process flow. The question has a defined set of alternative answers which are in effect, gates.

There are 4 types of gateways in BPMN

- Exclusive OR (XOR) Gateways
- AND Parallel Forking and Joining Gateways
- Inclusive OR Gateways
- Complex Decisions and Merges

Exclusive OR (XOR) Gateway Notations

 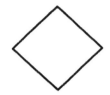

An *exclusive gateway* notation is depicted by a diamond shape with or without an X.

The *exclusive OR gateway* is considered an *OR (XOR) it* has specific results and instigates the way a process sequence flows. Exclusive means only one of many inputs or outputs is chosen from the gateway at any one time. This notation is the most commonly used gate throughout business process flows. The gate will merge 2 or more input sequence flows and produce one specific output flow. The *exclusive merging (XOR) gateway* is used to model a data-base merge.

Example of an Exclusive OR Merging Gateway

In the following example, the three inputs merge together at the *Exclusive Gateway,* which only allows one of the tasks A, B or C to continue to flow to task D at any one time.

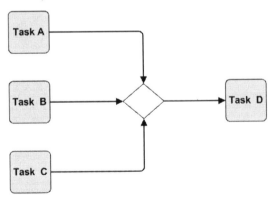

Diagram - Exclusive OR merging gateway

Conditional Flow Notation

Conditional flows are depicted by a diamond shape at one end of the connector and a solid arrowhead at the other end. Conditional flows are used when specific conditions are met at a decision gate. The decision gate routes the direction of the process sequence flow.

Default Sequence Flow Notation

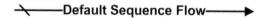

Default sequence flows are depicted by a small cross line at one end of the connector and a solid arrowhead at the other end. Default sequence flows are used when no other conditions are met.

Data-Based XOR Gateway

The data-based XOR gateway has the same effect as the exclusive OR (XOR) gateway however, in reverse. The sequence flow coming into the gate can take only one of the outputs. The expression at the gateway will decide which leg of the gateway is taken. This type of gateway can be drawn with or without an X in the middle.

Data-based XOR decisions are the most common XOR gateways used.

Example of a Data-Based XOR Gateway

In the following example, task A input splits at the data-based XOR into three branches.

The output path is chosen, depending on the conditions of each branch of the gateway.

The example shows three outputs:

- Always Condition
- Alternative
- Default Alternative

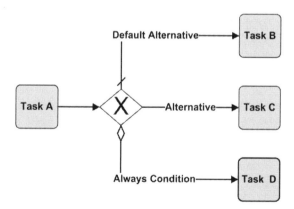

Diagram - Data-based XOR gateway

AND Parallel Forking and Joining Gateway Notation

 A *parallel gateway notation* is shown as a diamond shape with a plus sign in the centre.

Example of an AND Parallel Forking Gateway

The *parallel forking gateway* is also called an AND gateway. All sequence flows which branch out of the AND gateway are used.

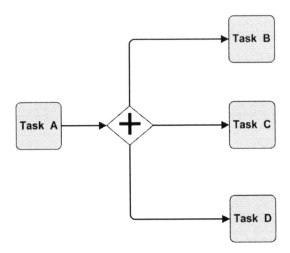

Diagram - AND parallel forking gateway

Example of an AND Parallel Joining Gateway

The *parallel joining gateway* must receive an input from all input sequence flows, for the output flow to be used. The process flow waits for all inputs to arrive at the AND gateway before continuing.

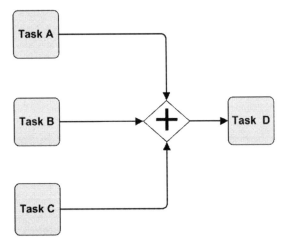

Diagram - AND parallel joining gateway

Inclusive OR Gateway Notation

An *inclusive OR gateway notation is shown as* a diamond shape containing a circle.

Example of an Inclusive OR Merging Gateway

The *inclusive OR merging gateway* signifies that the process flow continues when the first input arrives from any of the set of input sequence flows. If other inputs subsequently arrive from other input sequence flows, they are not used. The following example shows the sequence flow from three different tasks merging into an inclusive OR gateway.

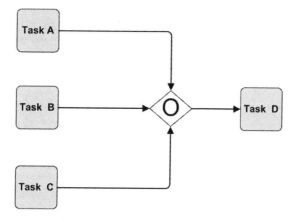

Diagram - Inclusive OR merging gateway

Example of an Inclusive OR Decision Gateway

The *inclusive OR decision gateway* allows the outgoing sequence flows from the gateway to be used depending on the condition. When no decision is made by the gate the output will take the default sequence flow. The following example shows the sequence flow from task A branching to tasks, depending on the gateway decision.

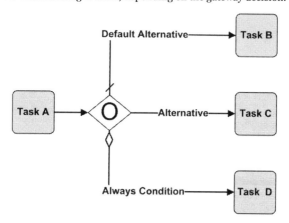

Diagram - Inclusive OR decision gateway

Complex Gateway Notation

A *complex gateway* notation is shown as a diamond shape containing a merged plus and a cross symbol together.

Example of a Complex Decision Gateway

The *complex decision gateway* is a specific complex flow condition that references outgoing sequence flow names. The *complex decision* gateway determines which output flow is to be taken.

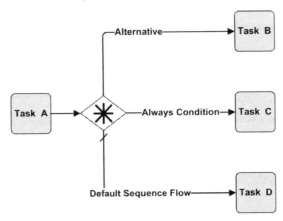

Diagram - Complex decision gateway

Example of a Complex Merging Gateway

The *complex merging gateway* is a specific complex flow condition which references incoming sequence flow names and/or process data that is coming into the gateway. The expression determines when the output process starts.

The *complex merging gateway* determines which one of the inputs flow from task A, task B, or task C to task D.

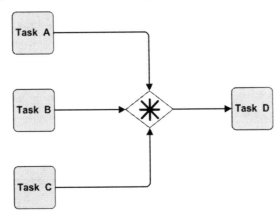

Diagram - Complex merging gateway

Exercise – gateways

Using the diagram *select and book vacation, on page 22* list which types of gateways were useod.

Could a default sequence flow have been used?

Process Pools and Swimlanes

Pools

Pools allow the process modeller to focus on a single business organisation and are considered *self-contained processes.*

Process Pool Notation

A *pool* is represented by a rectangle, either horizontally or vertically. A *pool* name is on the left side for a horizontal pool and on top for a vertical pool.

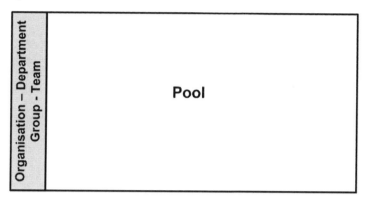

- A *pool* represents a single business organisation e.g. company, department or group and are normally used if the diagram involves two or more separate business entities

- *Pools* are graphical containers used to partition a set of activities

- The sequence flow of the process is contained within the *pool* and cannot cross the boundaries of the *pool*

- A *pool* acts as a container for a process, representing a participant in a business process diagram

.

Multi Instance Pool Notation

A *multi instance pool* notation is represented by a rectangle either horizontally or vertically, containing three parallel vertical lines in the bottom centre.

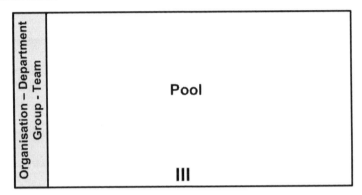

A *multi instance pool* is used when two or more of the same pool processes are performed simultaneously.

Swimlanes Notation

Swimlanes are sub-partitions within a pool and extend the entire length of the pool, vertically or horizontally, the same as the parent pool.

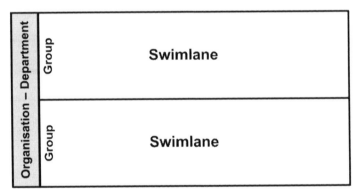

Swimlanes are used to organise and categorise activities of departments, groups or teams etc. which make up the total process within the pool.

Modelling a Simple Business Process

Business processes can be complex, however broken down into individual processes they can be defined in such a way that they are easily understood. Many departments are involved in different processes, however any process documentation should only reflect the involvement in the selected process.

A business process can be specific to only one department although, usually departments are involved in a multitude of different processes throughout a company.

The Process of Acquiring a Workstation

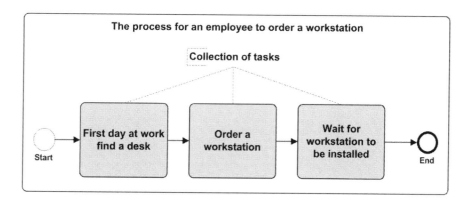

Diagram – Acquiring a workstation

In this example, an employee communicates with the IT support department.

- The first step in the process requires the employee, on the first day of work, to find a desk
- The next step is to order a workstation
- Wait for the workstation to be installed

Communication between two different departments

When a workstation is required, an employee is only responsible for the ordering of a workstation and has no direct involvement with IT support.

The following is a specific business process for requesting a workstation for a new employee. There are two different departments involved

A. The department of the new employee

B. The IT support department

The departments need to interact between each other to accomplish the process outcome.

Department requesting a workstation

The following is a business process diagram using BPMN task notations and shows the sequence of tasks when a workstation is requested for a new employee.

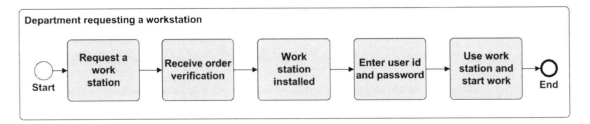

Diagram – Department requesting a workstation

- A request for a workstation for a new employee is sent to the IT department
- The employee receives an acknowledgment that the workstation has been requested
- The workstation is installed
- The employee enters a user id / password
- The employee uses the workstation

IT support department

Below is a business process diagram using BPMN task notations and shows the steps taken by the IT support department when a workstation is requested for a new employee.

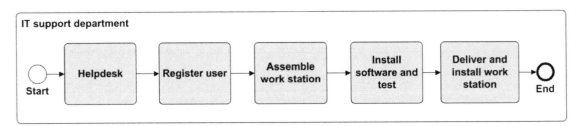

Diagram - IT support department

- The IT support helpdesk receives a request for a workstation and the relevant software to be installed for a new employee
- The new employee is registered and informed of the estimated delivery time
- The workstation is assembled and tested
- The specific software is installed and tested
- The workstation is delivered and installed

The Communication between two Entities

The *IT support department* process runs parallel with the department *requesting a workstation* process. It is necessary to show the communication between the *IT support department* and the department of the new employee. These are separate departments and therefore do not have a sequence flow connecting them.

The department *requesting a workstation* is not part of the *IT support department* therefore any communication between them takes the form of messages. This is called a *collaboration process*. The interaction of the tasks between the two departments is a flow of messages and data objects, such as emails, faxes, letters etc and is called a *message flow*

Message Sequence Flow

In the previous example, the department of the new employee interacts during the sequence flow with different groups, within the *IT support department.*

Both the department of the new employee and the *IT support department* are shown in two separate pools, which can only interact using a message sequence flow.

Note that the individual pools have a process sequence flow.

Message Flow Notation

Message flows are used to show the flow of messages between two or more pools. Message flows connect either to the pool boundary or directly to flow objects within the pool boundary.

○— — — — **Message Flow** — — —▷

A *Message Flow* is depicted by a dashed line with an open arrowhead at one end and an open circle at the other end. *Message Flows are* used to show the flow of messages between two separate process participants (business entities or business roles). *Message Flows* enable the analyst to model the order of tasks or sub-processes between organisations or departments in different pools.

Example of Communication between two Pools

The following is a business process diagram (BPD) depicted using BPMN tasks and describes the communication between the *department requesting a new workstation* with the *IT support department*.

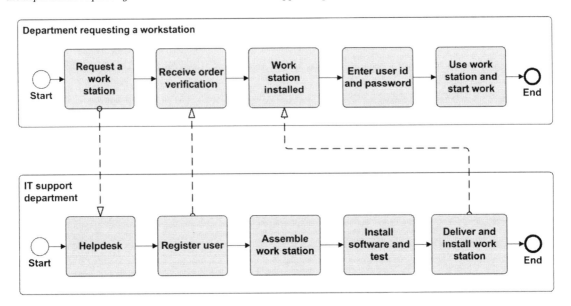

Diagram – Communication between two pools

- The request for a workstation is sent to the helpdesk as a message flow, which might be in the form of an email, an internal mail or a phone call, depending on how the organisation is set up
- The help desk registers the new user and responds with a user acknowledgement, providing confirmation that the request has been processed and the employee will receive a workstation
- The *IT support department* assembles and tests the workstation
- The software is installed, configured and tested
- A user id and password is provided

IT Support Department

The company *IT support department* can be further broken down into three different groups which are represented by swimlanes

- IT Service Desk which receives the request and registers the user

- Hardware support which assembles and tests the workstation

- Software Support which installs and tests the software

AS the *IT Support* has a requirement for a new workstation all groups within the department become involved in some part of the process sequence.

The following is a BPD using a *pool* and three *swimlanes* describing the business process of IT Support from receipt of the request to delivery and installation of a new workstation.

- Each group of the *IT department* is shown in its own *swimlane*

- The groups are shown in the same *pool* with different sets of tasks

- The individual groups have tasks that do not affect the other groups

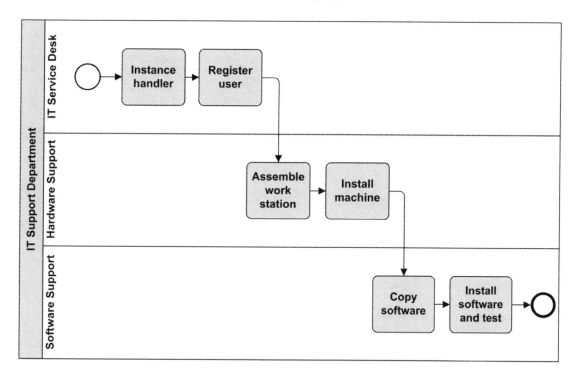

Diagram – IT support department swimlanes

Collaboration Processes

A *collaboration process* is when two different entities communicate with each other. Message events and message flows are used for this purpose with BPMN. Messages are sent and received to and from other processes in different pools enabling information to flow between pools.

Message Events

In a previous example, a message was used to communicate between the *department of the new employee* and the *IT support*. A further extension of the message flow is the use of *message events*. These events allow the modeller to depict when a message should occur and what the message is used for.

The following describes the type of *message events* that can be used for communicating with external entities.

Message Start Event Notation

Message start event notations are represented by an envelope inside a single thin circle.

Message start event notations are used to start a sequence on receiving a message from another pool.

Message Intermediate Event Notations

There are two notations depicting *message intermediate events* which are only used during the sequence flow, to show some form of message has been sent or received. *Message intermediate event* notations are represented by an envelope inside two thin circles.

Message intermediate catching evens notations are represented by a non filled envelope.

Message intermediate catching event notations are used to show that the process sequence flow is being prevented from continuing until a message has been received.

Message intermediate throwing event notations are represented by a filled envelope.

Message intermediate throwing event notations are used to show that a message has been sent during the sequence flow but is not prevented from continuing.

Message End Event Notation

Message end event notations are represented by a filled envelope inside a thick circle.

Message end event notations are used to send a message when the process sequence flow has ended.

Receive Task Initiating a Process Notation

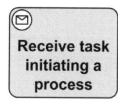

Receive task initiating a process notations are shown by a rectangle with rounded corners containing a message start event notation in the upper left corner.

The *receive task initiating a process* does not require an incoming sequence flow and indicates that the process sequence will be started by a message received. If the *receive task initiating a process* references a message, there is only one data output. If a data output is referenced, it must be the same as the message defined by the incoming associated message.

BPMN Data Object Notation

BPMN *data object* notation (commonly called an artefact) is utilised in a BPD for any type of data that needs to be part of a diagram. The *data object* can also be used as a message description between two process pools. A *data object* notation symbolises documents or data which are the results of activities and tasks.

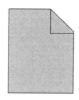

Data object notations are represented by a small rectangle with a folded corner in the top right hand side.

BPMN Association Notations

An *association notation* is represented by a dotted line with or without an arrowhead.

An *association notation* is used to link information and artefacts with flow objects.

It is used with the *data object* notation.

Collaboration Process

The diagram below shows an example of a collaboration process between the *department requesting a workstation* and *IT support department.*

- The overall process is started with a general unspecified *start event* from the department requesting a workstation pool
- IT Support pool begins the sequence flow with a *message start event*, and the *IT service desk* (swimlane) receiving a request for a new workstation
- After the user is registered, a message is sent to the department requesting the workstation using a *message intermediate throwing event*
- After the workstation is installed a confirmation m*essage* is sent to the department requesting the workstation.
- The department requesting a workstation sequence, waits for the confirmation message (Workstation installed), using a *message intermediate catching event*
- The department requesting the workstation sequence flow, ends with a *general end event*
- The IT Support sequence ends with a *message end event* sent to confirm workstation delivery

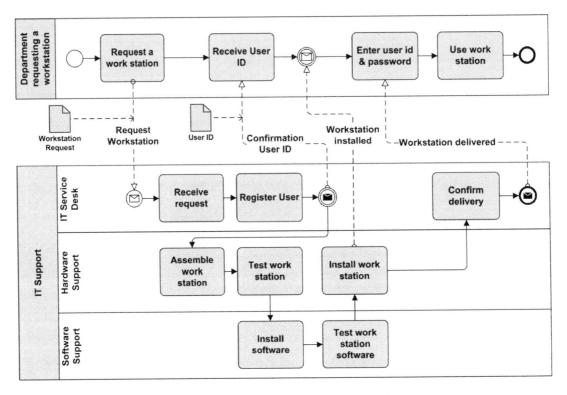

Diagram - Collaboration process using two pools

Question: What other notation could be used instead of the Receive request?

BPMN Course Book

BPMN Link Event Notations

In an internal BPD the *intermediate link event* notation can be used to make a link, without cluttering the diagram with a long, connecting sequence flow. *Link intermediate event notations* are always used in pairs, *source* intermediate event and *target* intermediate event.

The *intermediate link source event* notation is represented by a black arrow within two thin circles (throwing event). The *link intermediate throwing event* is the source of the link and shows the start of the link.

The *intermediate link target event* notation is represented by a white arrow within two thin circles (catching event). The *link intermediate catching event* is the target of the link and shows the link destination.

The throwing and catching events are a pair as one cannot be used without the other. Using *intermediate links* is just as useful as using the Go To symbols of a classical flowchart. They allow the process modeller to link a sequence output to a sequence input, without drawing a line. This is very useful in a complex diagram, when drawing a line would clutter the diagram. When using pairs of intermediate link notations, it is useful to designate them both with the same letter or number where more than one pair of links are used.

Black Boxes and White Boxes

There are times while modelling processes, when it is not required to know how a process works in another company, or department. In these circumstances, a company can be represented by a **black box** pool where there are no activities or tasks modelled. In contrast, **white box** pools have tasks and activities which are described in detail.

At some point in a process sequence, there is interaction between a **black box** pool and a **white box** pool using message flows and data objects such as emails, faxes, letters etc.

Collaboration Process Using Black Boxes

An example of a collaboration process is shown in the following diagram. The information is drawn from the previous diagram, *collaboration process using two pools*, showing a *black box* pool replacing, the *requesting a workstation* pool, and introducing a new *black box* pool representing a *Hardware supplier*.

IT support is shown as a *white box* and depicts the tasks and sequence flow of the IT support process.

Example of a Collaboration Process using Black Boxes

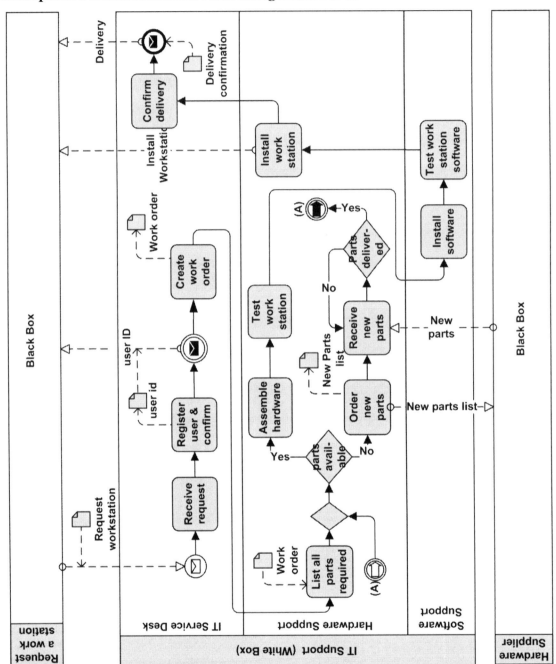

Diagram – Collaboration process using black boxes

Description of a Collaboration process using black boxes

The *IT Support* process sequence begins with a message start event, and the *IT service desk* receiving a request for a workstation, from the *requesting a workstation* process black box pool.

The user of the *requesting a workstation* process is registered by the *IT service desk*. A confirmation is created and returned to the *requesting a workstation* black box process pool, through a message flow.

The *IT service desk* creates a work order which is passed to *hardware support*. *Hardware support* checks that all parts are available.

If all parts are available, the sequence proceeds to assemble the workstation and test workstation tasks.

If parts are unavailable, a list of parts to be ordered is documented and shown as a *data object* notation. The parts' list is sent via a message flow to the Hardware supplier, shown as a black box pool.

Hardware support waits until new parts are delivered by the hardware supplier. When the hardware supplier delivers the parts, as shown by a message flow, *Hardware support* continues assembling the workstation and testing.

When the workstation is assembled and tested, the process sequence continues to *Software support* for software installation and testing.

The *Hardware support* process sequence continues with the installation of the workstation and informs the *requesting a workstation* black box process pool.

IT service desk prepares and sends a confirmation shown as a data object, to the user of the *requesting a workstation* process in the form of a message and the *IT support* process finishes with an end message event.

In the BPD, a *intermediate link* pair is depicted to prevent cluttering the diagram. The *intermediate link* pair make the connection from (A) *parts have arrived* (source event) to (A) *all parts available* (target event).

Notes

Exercise - collaboration process

From a previous process diagram 'Select and book vacation' on page 22, remodel the process using pools. At least two of the tasks communicate with another process pool using message events and data objects.

Messages and Conversations

A message represents the content of a communication between two participant pools in a collaboration process. In collaboration diagrams, a message flow symbol is included to show that a message is passed from one participant pool to another.

There two different types of messages

Initiating Message Notation

 An *initiating message* notation is depicted by an unfilled envelope drawn with a single thin line.

Non-Initiating Message Notation

 A *non-initiating message* notation is depicted by a lightly shaded envelope drawn with a single thin line.

Initiating Message Flow Notation

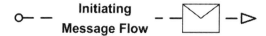

Initiating message flow notations are depicted by a dashed line with an open arrowhead at one end and an unfilled envelop denoting the start of a message.

None Initiating Message Flow Notation

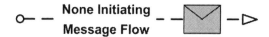

None initiating message flow notations are depicted by a dashed line with an open arrowhead at one end and a lightly shaded envelope denoting a message response.

Example of a Message Exchange

The following diagram describes the interaction using messages between two participating pools i.e. a customer and a supplier. The message flow is only used between two external pools. The *initiating message* is sent by the customer pool and the responding n*on-initiating message* is sent by the supplier.

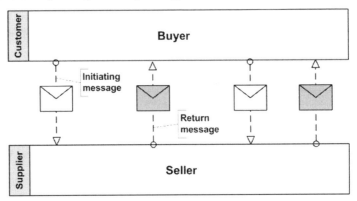

Diagram – Message exchange

Example of a Message Flow

The following diagram represents a simple collaboration message flow.

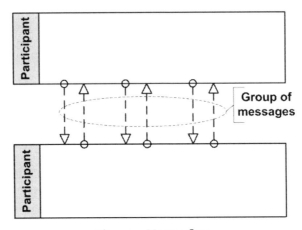

Diagram – Message flow

Exercise - Message flows

Give an example of a group of messages

-
-
-
-

Conversation Link Notation

A *conversation link* notation is depicted by two thin parallel lines. *Conversation links are* used in conjunction with *conversation nodes* to describe a set of message flows between two participants in a collaboration process. Two or more pools can use the *conversation link* with a *conversation node* describing types of conversations.

Conversation Node Notation

A *conversation node* notation is a hexagon drawn with a thin single line. The *conversation node* is used to represent a set of message exchanges and represents a message flow grouped together based on a specific concept e.g. order, order confirmation and delivery note. The *conversation node* always involves two or more participant process pools.

Example of a Conversation Node

The following diagram shows a *conversation node* depicting a message flow.

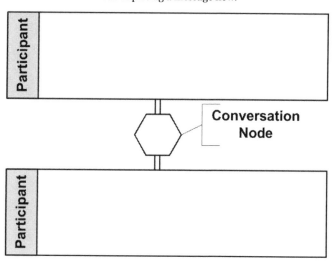

Diagram – Conversation node

Exercise – Conversation node

Using the previous exercise *message flows*, what would be written on the conversation node to describe the message flow?

Example of a Conversation Node with Message Flows

The following diagram shows two pairs of message flows as well as a conversation node, between two participants.

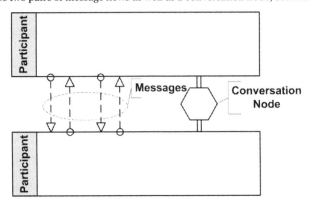

Diagram – Conversation node with message flows

Sub-Conversation Node Notation

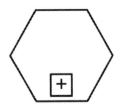

A *sub-conversation node* notation is shown as a hexagon drawn with a thin line containing a square with a plus sign (+) bottom centre. The *sub-conversation node* is used within a collaboration process replacing message flows and conversations.

Example of a Sub-Conversation Node

The following example shows the *sub-conversation* notation used to include different message flows and or conversation nodes

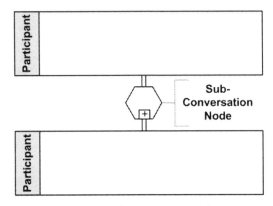

Diagram – Sub-conversation node

Global Call Conversation Notation

A *global call conversation* node notation is a hexagon drawn with a thick line. The *global call conversation* identifies a place in the conversation where a global conversation is required.

Collaboration Call Conversation Notation

A *collaboration call conversation* node notation is shown as a hexagon drawn with a thick line containing a small square with a plus sign (+) marker bottom centre. The collaboration *call conversation* is used to call a collaboration process.

Notes

Artefacts

Data Object Notations

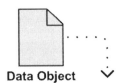

Data Object

Data object notations are represented by a small rectangle with a turned over corner in the top right hand side.

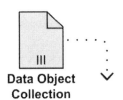

Data Object Collection

Data collection object notations are represented by a small rectangle with a turned over corner in the top right hand side with the addition of three lines at the bottom, depicting a collection of documents.

Data objects are used to show how data is required or produced by activities. The *data object* can be anything that is regarded as a data element i.e. letter, paper invoice, email, excel or word documents etc. The *data object collection* describes a collection of documents.

Data Input Notations

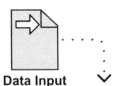

Data Input

Data input notations are represented by a rectangle with a turned over corner in the top right hand side and a non filled arrow in the top left corner.

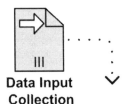

Data Input Collection

Data input collection notations are represented by a rectangle with a turned over corner in the top right hand side and a non filled arrow in the top left corner and three horizontal lines bottom centre.

Data Output Notations

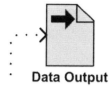

Data Output

Data output notations are represented by a rectangle with a turned over corner in the top right hand side and a filled arrow in the top left corner.

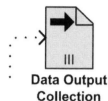

Data Output Collection

Data output collection notations are represented by a rectangle with a turned over corner in the top right hand side and a filled arrow in the top left corner and three horizontal lines bottom centre.

Data notations depict information produced by tasks specifically as an output, to be available for other tasks and sub-processes as an input. The *data association* helps to describe the direction of the data and which element it is attached to.

Examples of Data Objects

The following example demonstrates using a *data object* as a single input and a *data object collection* as a collection of documents as output from a task or sub-process. The *data object* has an association with an arrow to show the connection to the task or sub-process

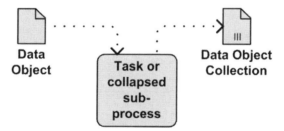

The following example demonstrates using a d*ata input* object as a single input to a task or sub-process and a *data output collection* object as a collection of output documents from the task or sub-process.

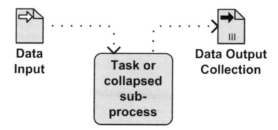

Group Notation

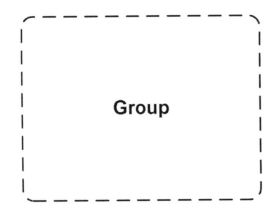

A *group* notation is represented by a rounded corner rectangle drawn with a dashed line. The *group* is used for documentation or analytic purposes, and does not affect the sequence flow. The *group* notation is used to describe groups of tasks or sub-processes, which are part of the same operation, and are required to be performed in a specific manor.

Annotation Notation

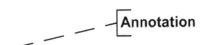

An *annotation* notation is represented by a three sided partial box, containing the required information. The associated line is dashed without an arrow. *The annotation notation is* a mechanism for modellers to provide additional text information for the reader of a BPD.

Data Store Notation

Data store notations are depicted as a cylinder with two lines around the top. A *data store* provides a source of data for activities to retrieve data or store data. A *data association* can be shown by an arrow to describe the direction of the data.

Question: What connection would be used to show data being stored and retrieved from the *data store* artefact?

Modelling using BPMN Events

Business Events are a relatively recent addition to process modelling. BPMN provides a rich list of very usable event notations which allows the user to specify a more exact sequence flow.

An event is an incident that takes place during the course of a business process and is used to control the process sequence. Events affect the flow of the process and usually have a cause (trigger) and an impact (result). There are three types of events used based on when they affect the flow, *start*, *intermediate* and *end*. BPMN provides a distinct notation for each of these types of events.

Specifying a type of event puts certain constraints on the process flow that is being modelled, for example, a timer event cannot end a process flow. These types of modelling rules, which can be classified as business rules, may be enforced automatically by the modelling tool providing support for BPMN.

Start Events

Anytime a business process begins there must be something which initiates the process sequence. In BPMN terminology, this is called a *start event*. A *start event* should describe what triggers the sequence flow. For example, if it is a timer event, then the annotation could be, 'the 'alarm clock rings at 7 am Monday through Friday'.

Interrupt and Non-interrupt Start Events

A *start event* is used to start a top level process sequence, an interrupting sub-process or non-interrupting sub-process. The sub-process start event interrupts the sequence flow and returns when the sub-process has been completed. If the sub-process start event is a non-interrupting start event, the top level sequence flow continues while the sub-process proceeds, thus not interrupting the top level sequence.

Start events can be used to

- start a process when a message is received (Page 38)
- start a process at a specific time or date
- start a process when a specific condition occurs
- start a process when multiple events occur

Modelling Using Business Intermediate Events

Intermediate events are one of the more unfamiliar items in BPMN. They allow for some of the cleanest, unambiguous expressions of steps in business processes. As the name implies, the *intermediate event* indicates where an event happens between the start and end of a process. It will affect the flow of the process, but will not start or directly terminate the process.

Intermediate events can be used to

- show where messages are expected or sent within the process
- show where delays are expected within the process
- show where the sequence flow will be controlled under certain conditions
- show where the sequence flow will be continued by another process
- show where the sequence flow of another process can be started or continued

The intermediate events that are used as part of the sequence flow do not start or stop the sequence flow but allow the modeller to design an event between tasks or sub-processes. There are six standard types of intermediate events that can be included in a BPD model.

- The unspecified / *none intermediate event* can be used when the modeller requires an event for diagramming purposes
- The *message intermediate event* receives or sends a message to another process without stopping the flow (page 38)
- The *timer intermediate event* temporarily stops the sequence until the date and time are relevant
- The *conditional intermediate event* allows continuation of the sequence flow if the condition is satisfied
- *The parallel multiple intermediate event* controls the sequence flow until all the events specified, occur
- The *multiply intermediate event* allows some or all of the immediate events to be specified by one event

Unspecified / None Intermediate Event Notation

An *unspecified / none intermediate event* notation is depicted by two circles one drawn inside the other.

The *unspecified intermediate event* does not have a specific purpose but can be used in a variety of ways to detail a diagram. The *unspecified intermediate event* is only used within the process sequence flow.

Example of a None or Unspecified Intermediate Event

In the following example, invoices are checked and are sent to the customer. The *unspecified / none intermediate event* shows that at this point in the sequence flow, the invoices are all completed.

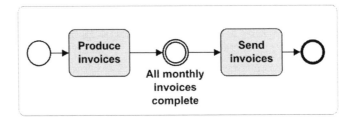

Diagram - Unspecified / none intermediate event

Timer Events

Timer Start Event Notations

 A *timer start event* notation is a catching event and is depicted by a circle containing a clock face.

 A *timer start event* notation used as a non-interrupt catching event is depicted with a dashed circle containing a clock face.

The *timer start event* when used in a sub-process can be an interruptible or a non-interruptible event. The *timer start event* is used to start a process at a specific time/date. A specific time/date or a specific cycle (e.g., every Monday at 9am) can be set that will trigger the start of the process. It can also be used for processes that repeat on a schedule (hourly, daily, etc). If in the pervious process of *going to work*, the sequence was started by the alarm clock going off, then the *timer start event* could have been used.

Example of a Timer Start Event

The following example shows the *timer start event* triggering the process of checking customer orders from 10:00 which takes into account the post delivery.

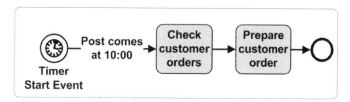

Diagram – Timer start event

Timer Intermediate Event Notation

 A *timer intermediate catching event* notation is depicted by two circles drawn one inside the other containing a clock face.

By using this event the sequence flow is stopped until a time, a date, or a recurring time or date allows the continuation of the process sequence flow. A specific time/date or a specific cycle (e.g., every Monday at 9am) can be set that will trigger the event. If the timer event is triggered, then this is considered a catching event.

Example of a Timer Intermediate Event

In the following example, the invoices are checked but the *timer intermediate event* only allows the sequence to continue at 16:00 when the invoices are sent to be posted.

Diagram – Timer intermediate event

Question: Could another start event be used?

Conditional Events

Conditional Start Event Notations

A *conditional start event* notation is a catching event and is depicted by a circle containing a rectangle with horizontal lines.

A *conditional start event* notation used as a *non-interrupt catching event* is depicted by a dashed circle containing a rectangle with horizontal lines.

The *conditional start event* when used in a sub-process can be an interruptible or non-interruptible event. The *conditional start event* is triggered when a specific condition occurs.

Example of a Conditional Start Event

The following example shows a *Conditional Start Event* triggering the process of 10 or more articles, ordered.

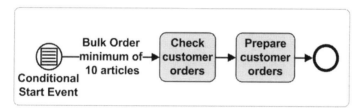

Diagram – Conditional start event

Question: What condition could be used to give the opposite effect?

Conditional Intermediate Event Notation

 A *conditional intermediate catching event* notation is depicted by two circles containing a rectangle with horizontal lines.

This type of event is triggered when a specific condition becomes valid. The evaluation of a condition initiates the continuation of that part of the process.

Example of a Conditional Intermediate Catching Event

In the following example, the invoices are checked and paid if they are due.

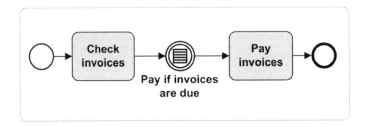

Diagram – Conditional intermediate catching event

Parallel Multiple Events

Parallel Multiple Start Event Notations

A *parallel multiple start event* notation is a catching event and is depicted by a circle containing an unfilled plus sign.

A *parallel multiple start event* notation used as a *non-interrupt catching event* is depicted by a dashed circle containing an unfilled plus sign.

The *parallel multiple start event* when used in a sub-process can be an interruptible or a non-interruptible event. The *parallel multiple start event* is triggered when two or more different types of start events occur at the same time.

Example of a Parallel Multiple Start Event

In the following example, the task *Receive customer order* will only start after 09:00 even though an order could arrive much earlier.

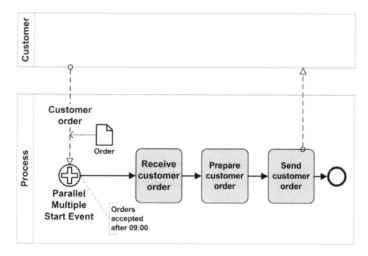

Diagram – Parallel multiple start event

Question: What are the events used in this example?

Parallel Multiple Intermediate Catching Event Notation

A *parallel multiple intermediate catching event* notation is depicted by two circles drawn one inside the other, containing an unfilled plus sign.

The *parallel multiple intermediate catching event* is triggered when a group of several different events occur at the same time, in order for the process flow to continue.

Any intermediate catching event can be included as part of the *parallel multiple intermediate events*.

Example of a Parallel Multiple Intermediate Catching Event

In the following example, invoices are checked and if due, and it is the end of the month, they are paid.

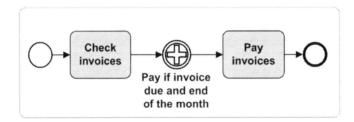

Diagram - Parallel multiple intermediate catching event

Question: Which events are used in this example?

Multiple Events

Multiple Start Event Notations

A *multiple start event* notation is a catching event and is depicted by a circle containing a pentagon.

A *multiple start event* notation used as a *non-interrupt catching event* is depicted with a dashed circle containing a pentagon.

The *multiple start event* when used in a sub-process can be an interruptible or a non-interruptible event. *The multiple start event* can be triggered by receiving any combination of a message start event, a timer start event, conditional start event or a signal start event. *The multiple start event* allows multiple methods of triggering the process however, only one of them is required to start the process. A business process may be initiated by more than one start trigger.

In the process of *going to work* from a previous diagram, the start event could have two possibilities

a. woken up by someone

b. an alarm clock going off

If either could trigger the start then a Multiple Start Event could be used.

Example of a Multiple Start Event

In the following example, the task 'Receive customer order' is triggered, either by receiving the order by email or the morning post at 10:00.

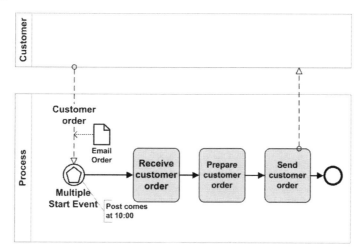

Diagram - Multiple start event

Question: If the process requires that the task Receive customer order is started at 10:00 even if an email order has been received, what start event could be used?

Multiple Intermediate Caching Event Notation

 A *multiple intermediate catching event* notation is depicted by two circles one drawn inside the other with thin lines, containing unfilled pentagon

A *multiple intermediate catching event* when used in a sequence flow waits for any of the designated triggers before continuing the sequence flow. This is considered a catching event because it responses to a trigger from another process, time or condition. The *multiple intermediate catching event* is used when more than one type of event occurs during the sequence flow.

Example of a Multiple Intermediate Catching Event

In the following example, invoices are checked and paid if due or if it is the end of the month.

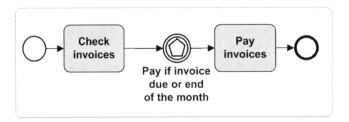

Diagram - Multiple intermediate catching event

Question: What are the events used in the above diagram?

Multiple Intermediate Throwing Event Notation

A *multiple intermediate throwing event* notation is depicted by two circles, one drawn inside the other, containing a filled pentagon.

When used in a sequence flow, the *multiple intermediate throwing event* does not change or stop the flow but causes a trigger to be sent to other processes.

The *multiple intermediate throwing event* will throw all events specified, at the same time and can only include:

- Message event
- Compensation event
- Signal throwing event

Example of a Multiple Intermediate Throwing Event

In the following example an order is received from a customer. If parts are unavailable, an order is sent to a parts supplier at the same time as a signal is sent to purchasing, to update ordered records. This event shows that there are multiple triggers assigned to the event which can *throw* all of the designated triggers. This makes for a cleaner diagram however it is an advantage to describe all the different triggers.

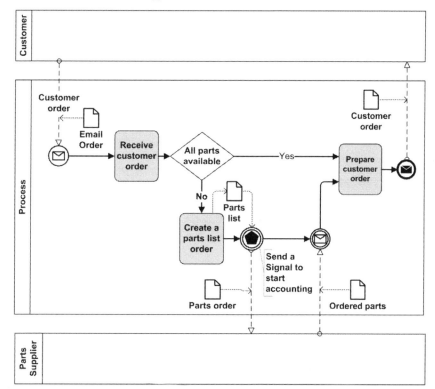

Diagram - Multiple intermediate throwing event

Signal events are described in a later chapter

End Events

Sometime, somehow, a process sequence must be completed. Often the completion of one process can initiate another business process. In BPMN terminology, this is called an *end event* and is used to stop the process sequence.

Multiple Intermediate End Event Notation

A *multiple end event* notation is a throwing event and is depicted by a circle containing a filled pentagon.

The *multiple end event* provides a method of simplifying diagrams while specifying that more than one type of end event occurs at the completion of a process.

Example of a Multiple End Event

In the following example, the process begins with a message start event triggered by receiving an order from a customer. The customer order is processed and the process sequence is completed with a *Multiple End Event*, which shows not only an invoice being sent to the customer but also the product.

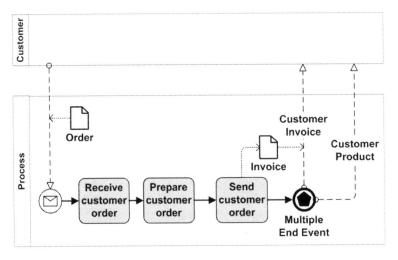

Diagram - Multiple end event

Question: What are the end events used in the above diagram?

Terminate End Event Notation

A *terminate end event* notation is depicted by a thick circle containing a large filled dot.

A *terminate end event* used in BPMN signifies that all activities in the process cease immediately. When this event is used in a sub-process, the whole inline process stops and does not continue with any other tasks or sub-processes. The terminate end event is the "stop everything" event and when reached, the entire process stops including all parallel processes and all instances of multi-instances. The process ends without compensation or event handling

Example of a Terminate End Event

In the following example, the process begins with a message start event triggered by receiving an order from a customer. The customer credit is checked and if not credit worthy, the sub-process and the inline process is terminated immediately. If the customer is credit worthy, the order is processed and the product and invoice are sent to the customer.

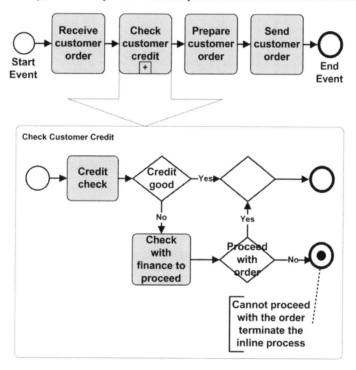

Diagram - Terminate end event

Event Based Gateways

Exclusive Event-Based XOR Gateway Notation

An *event-based XOR gateway* notation is shown as a diamond shape containing two thin circles surrounding a pentagon.

The *event-based XOR gateway* is used when multiple events merge or fork. The output of the gateway will depend on the decision of the gateway. Exclusive denotes that only one of many inputs or outputs is chosen to be the output from the gate, at any one time.

Merge Event-Based XOR Gateway

A merge *event-based XOR gateway* is used when only one output is permitted from multiple inputs.

Example of a Merge Event-Based XOR Gateway

In the following example, the three inputs merge together at the *event-based XOR gateway. The gateway* only allows one of the following inputs, task A, start message event or intermediate timer event to continue the sequence flow to task B, at any one time.

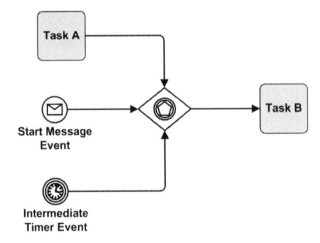

Diagram - Merge event-based XOR gateway

Fork Event-Based XOR Gateway

A *fork event-based XOR gateway* has the same effect as the *merge event-based XOR gateway* however, *in reverse*. The *fork event-based XOR gateway* controls the sequence flow coming into the gate and can take only one of the outputs. The expression at the gateway will decide which branch of the gateway is taken.

Example of a Fork Event-Based XOR Gateway

In the following example, task A output splits at the *fork event-based XOR gateway* into three branches task B, end *message event* or *intermediate timer event*. The output path is chosen based on conditions at each branch of the gateway.

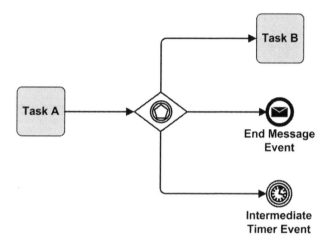

Diagram- Fork event-based XOR gateway

Question: List the branch conditions that could be used?

-

-

-

Modelling a Complete Business Process

Before starting to develop a new business process or improve an existing process it is necessary to create the required documentation. A Business Process Map needs to be developed before process modelling can begin. The Business Process Map must be comprehensive and understandable to all parties before proceeding further. It is very important that the documents are complete and reflect the business requirements.

In the following example, a Computer Hardware Supplier company documents a new process allowing customers to purchase products to order. The business process is called, **computer products to customer order**. The documentation describes how the business process, **computer products to customer order**, is to be executed within the framework of the business requirements.

The Business Process Map

The following constitutes a Business Process Map

1) Business process description

2) Business process overview

3) Business document flow

4) Business process sequence

Business Process Description

Business process name

        Computer products to customer order

Business process owner

        To be designated

Business process analyst

        To be designated

Business process overview

The company will produce computer products on demand for delivery within 15 working days. The customer is informed at all stages of the process i.e. confirmation of order, confirmation of delivery, delivery note and an invoice if applicable. Product parts will be either on stock or ordered from a parts manufacturer. After the products are assembled and tested, they are packed and delivered to the customer.

Sub-processes

1.   Receive and process order

2.   Assemble components and test

3.   Create invoice and delivery note

4.   Pack and ship product

Process description

The process starts with an order from a customer which is handled by the back office department. The back office department checks the customer credit rating and confirms acceptance of the order.

The customer order is reviewed by the back office and a work order created detailing the specific customer requirements.

The work order is checked for parts on stock and a confirmation of delivery is produced, informing the customer of the delivery schedule. The work order proceeds to product assembly and test department, where the required product is produced.

Once the product is ready, an invoice and a delivery note are prepared. The product is packed and shipped by an outsourced company.

Process trigger

The process is triggered by a customer order for computer products.

Process results

The products will be assembled, tested and delivered to the customer with an invoice to be paid within 30 days or COD.

Process inputs

- Customer detailed order email
- Customer detailed order fax

Process outputs

- Delivery schedule
- Computer products
- Delivery note
- Invoice

Process business rules

- The hardware will be delivered within 15 working days from order
- Customer receives an order confirmation within one working day
- Customer receives a product delivery schedule within three working days from order
- Customer is informed of any delays to the delivery schedule within two working days
- If the customer is credit worthy an invoice is sent when the product is ready to be shipped
- Invoice is included with the product and delivery note for COD payment if the customer is not credit worthy
- Outsource shipping company will have three days to deliver products

Process interfaces

- Customer
- Parts supplier
- Outsourced shipping company
- Finance department

Process notes

The process design is only concerned with the process sequence of the **Computer Hardware Supplier Co**. and not with any other entity, although there are interface requirements to other companies.

The finance department is required to respond and to advise on customer credit worthiness.

Business Process Overview

Upon completion of the Business Process Description, a Business Process Overview outlining the sub-process and the process timing is produced. The Business Process Overview shows collapsed sub-processes requiring a BPD to describe each sub-process.

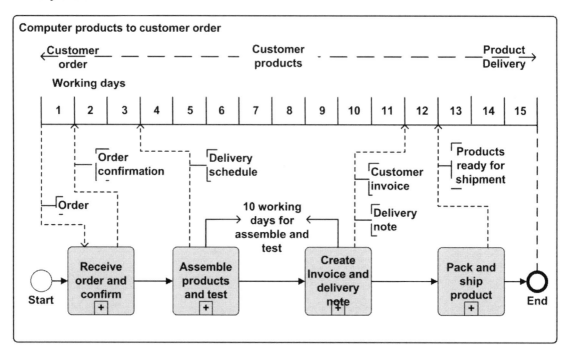

Diagram- Computer products to customer order

Business process overview description

The **computer products to customer order** process requires four sub-processes to complete the business process. Each sub-process follows in sequence, as one must be completed before the next starts. There is one input, **the customer order**, which is received by email or fax. The total time from order to product received by the customer, is a maximum of 15 working days.

Business process overview process timing

- The process timing shows that the products are ready for shipment three working days before the customer receives the products, to allow the shipping company time to deliver.

- The customer invoice and the delivery note are completed one day after receiving the completed work order.

- The **Assemble products and test** sub-process has a maximum of 10 working days to provide fully tested products. The timing will also depend on receiving the components ordered from the parts supplier.

- The delivery schedule is sent three days after receiving the customer requirements from the **Receive order and confirm** sub-process. The delivery schedule will depend on the estimated date of delivery from the parts supplier.

- The **Receive order and confirm** sub-process has one working day to check the order and send the confirmation to the customer, after receiving the customer order. During this time, the credit worthiness of the customer must be checked and the customer requirements document must be completed.

Business Process Document Flow

The Business Process Document Flow describes the process documents that are to be produced for the customer and also the required internal documents.

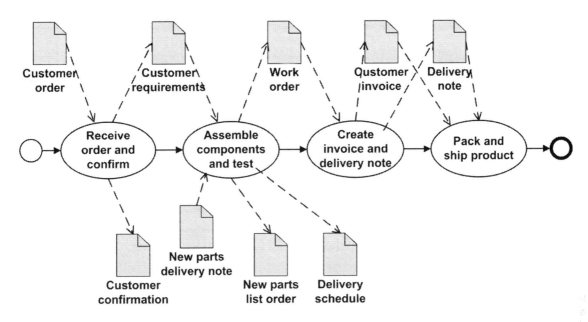

Diagram – Business process document flow

Business process document flow description

The **computer products to customer order** process produces four documents which are sent to the customer

- Customer order confirmation
- Delivery schedule
- Customer invoice
- Delivery note

Three internal documents

- Customer requirements
- Parts order used to request parts from the parts supplier
- Work order used as an internal document throughout the product assembly and testing

Business Process Sequence

The following BPD describes the business process sequence and where and when documents are an input and where documents are produced.

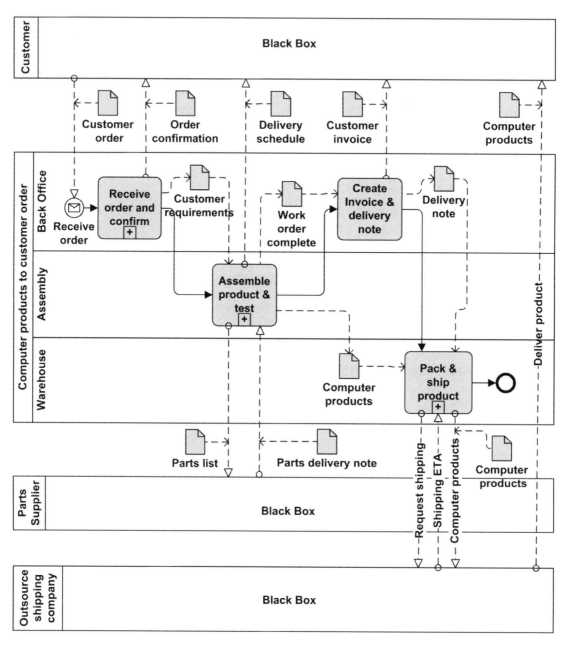

Diagram - Business Process Sequence

The business process sequence description

The **computer products to customer order** process is a white box pool and is broken into three specific swimlanes. The swimlanes represent the departments used in this process.

- back office
- assembly
- warehouse

Three process pools are designated as black box pools.

- outsourced shipping company
- parts supplier
- customer

The communication between the black box pools and the white box pool is shown using message flows.

The customer sends one document, customer order, which starts the process. The customer receives four different documents from the **computer products to customer order** process.

- order confirmation
- delivery schedule
- customer invoice
- delivery note (included in the product packaging)

If new parts are required the parts supplier receives a parts list, and responds with an estimated delivery time for the new parts. The estimated delivery time will enable the **computer products to customer order** process, to confirm the delivery schedule to the customer. The new parts will be supplied accompanied by a parts delivery note.

The outsourced shipping company is requested for an estimated time of arrival (ETA) which will influence the delivery time to the customer.

Modelling Business Sub-processes

The previous chapter documented the new business process **_Computer products to customer order_** to be developed for the Hardware Supplier Company. The following BPD shows the sub-processes required.

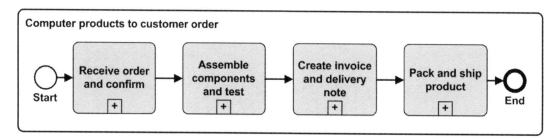

Diagram –Overview computer products to customer order

Receive order and confirm

Description

The process receives an order from a new or existing customer and checks the customer database. If the customer is new, the database is updated. The customer credit status is checked with the finance department before proceeding. If the customer has a good credit rating, an invoice will be sent on delivery of the products, otherwise the payment is COD. An order requirement is produced and passed to **Assemble components and test.**

Tasks

Receive and check for a valid order

Check customer database

Update customer database

Check credit

Check with finance to proceed

Create and send unable to complete order

Create and send confirmation of customer order

Create order requirements for assembly and payment

Trigger

Customer order

Inputs

Customer order

Outputs

Customer requirements

Business rules

If the customer is not credit worthy, then the finance department will advise whether the order can be completed COD.

If the finance department advises against completing the order, notification is sent to the customer.

Interfaces

Customer

Receive order and confirm (BPD)

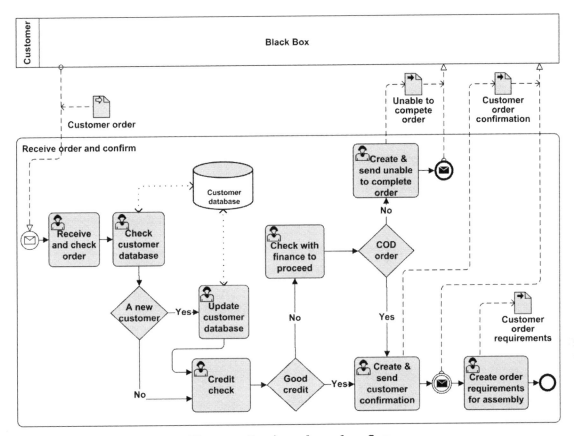

Diagram – Receive order and confirm

BPD description

- The order is received and the customer is checked on the database
- If customer credit is questionable, the finance department checks the credit rating before an order is processed
- If the credit check is positive, then the process continues with the order
- An order confirmation is sent to the customer and an order requirement is produced and sent to **Assemble components and test**
- If the credit is questionable, then the finance department advises whether to allow the order COD, otherwise the customer is informed the products cannot be delivered

Assemble components and test

Description

This sub-process accepts the order requirements, checks the parts availability, produces a work order and proceeds to assemble the product. After the product is tested it is moved to packaging and shipping.

N.B: If parts are not available, then the required parts are ordered. Testing could reveal bad components and therefore new components must be ordered.

Tasks

Check requirements and create a work order

Check order against inventory

Create delivery schedule

Assemble products

Create a new parts list order

Receive new parts

Test product (sub-process)

Deliver products to packaging

Trigger

Customer order requirements

Inputs

Order requirements document

Outputs

Computer products

Work order (completed)

Customer delivery schedule

Business rules

The computer products will be assembled and tested within 10 working days.

Customer is sent a product delivery schedule within two working days of receiving the order requirements.

Customer is informed of any delays to the delivery schedule within one working day.

Interfaces

Customer

Parts supplier

Assemble components and test BPD

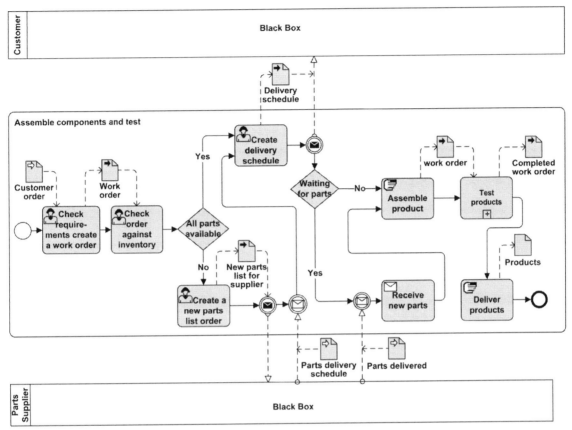

Diagram – Assemble components and test

BPD description

- The customer order requirements are checked and a work order is produced
- If any parts are not in stock, then further parts are ordered from the parts supplier
- The customer is sent a delivery schedule
- The products are assembled and sent for testing
- When the work order is completed it is sent to **Create invoice and delivery note**
- When the work order is completed the products are delivered to **Package product and ship goods**

Test products

Description

The computer products are tested for hardware and software errors.

Tasks

Receive assembled product

Check assembled product against work order

Run basic hardware tests

Remedy hardware failures

Run basic software tests

Check system for errors and correct

Trigger

A computer product is delivered with a work order

Inputs

Customer product

Work order

Outputs

Tested customer products

Business rules

The computer products are tested within 2 working days.

Interfaces

None

Exercise - Test products BPD

Use the information provided and model the sub-process   - *Test products*

Process name:

BPD description

- The products are received with a work order and are tested for hardware errors
- The products are tested with the ordered software

Create invoice and delivery note

Description

When the completed work order is received the customer invoice is produced along with the delivery note. If the customer is COD, then the invoice is provided with the delivery note to **Package product and ship goods,** otherwise the invoice is sent directly to the customer.

Tasks

Check work order against customer order

Create invoice

Create delivery note

Send invoice to customer

Forward invoice to warehouse

Forward delivery note to warehouse

Trigger

Completed work order

Inputs

Completed work order

Outputs

Invoice

Delivery note

Business rules

An invoice will be produced and sent to the customer within one working day of receiving the completed work order.

In the case of COD both the invoice and the delivery note will be sent to **Package product and ship goods**.

Interfaces

Customer

Create invoice and delivery note BPD

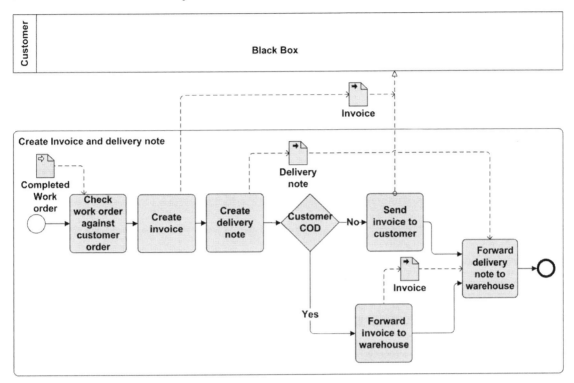

Diagram – Create invoice and delivery note

BPD description

- When a completed work order is received an invoice for the customer is produced along with a delivery note
- If the customer has a good credit rating the invoice is sent directly to the customer, otherwise it is forwarded to **Package product and ship goods**
- The delivery note is always sent to **Package product and ship goods**

Using the following table, list the tasks types used in sub-process **Create invoice and delivery note.**

Sub-process task list	Sub-process task type list
Check work order against customer order	
Create invoice	
Create delivery note	
Send invoice to customer	
Forward invoice to warehouse	
Forward delivery note to warehouse	

Table – Sub-process task list

Pack and ship product

Description

The product is packaged along with the delivery note. A shipping company is arranged and the goods handed over for delivery to the customer.

Tasks

Receive product

Collect specific packaging material

Package product with delivery note

Find best shipping company for destination

Order shipping company

Create bill of lading

Place product in finished goods

Check finished goods

Hand over all goods for shipment

Trigger

Computer products with delivery note

Inputs

Computer product

Delivery note

Invoice in the case of COD

Outputs

Packaged computer products with delivery note

Invoice with COD

Business rules

A shipping company is selected that can deliver the products on time, at the best price

Interfaces

Outsourced shipping company

Pack and ship product BPD

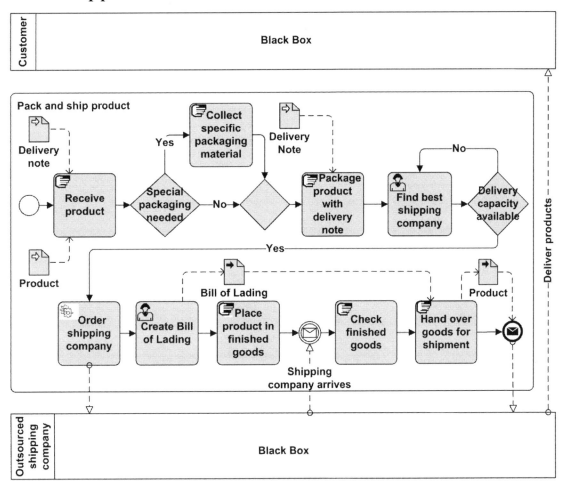

Diagram – Pack and ship product

BPD description

- The received product is packaged with the delivery note
- The appropriate shipping company is selected, that will deliver on time, at the best price
- When the shipping company arrives, the goods are handed over with a Bill of Lading

Exercise - Outsourced shipping company

The **Outsourced shipping company** process is modelled in the previous BDP as a black box pool. Using the diagram below model the relevant process of the **Outsourced shipping company** to interface with the Pack and ship product process.

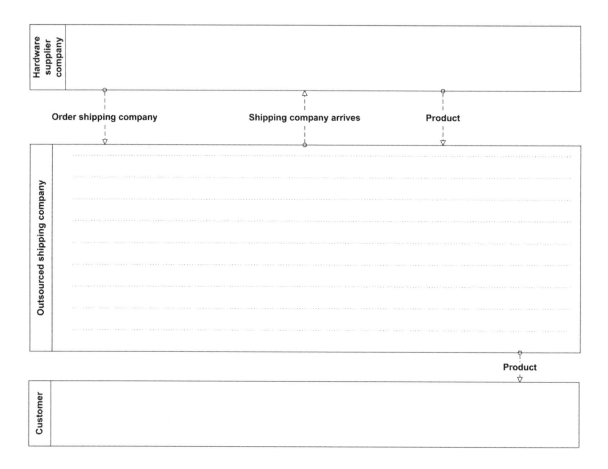

Granularity

Process decomposition is called **granularity** which describes different levels of diagrams depending on requirements. A top-level BPD is a sequence of collapsed sub-processes. Sub-processes can **decompose** without any restriction, therefore creating sub-processes for sub-processes, and so forth.

Further decomposition is an option, but too many sub-processes make the overall business process documentation complicated and therefore not user friendly and unmanageable. By using sub-processes it is easier to understand the overall diagram although the question should be asked, how far sub-processes should be broken-down into further sub-process (or **decomposed**).

Showing the details of a process, graphically, with another BPD is considered a **decomposed** process

Granularity Table

This granularity table is not a hard and fast rule but an example of what could be used.

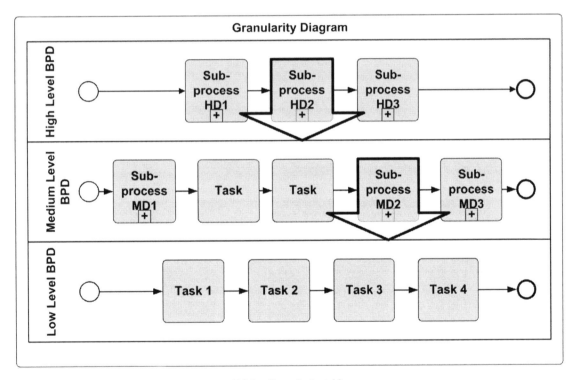

Table - Granularity table

Example of a Process Using Granularity

The process, **Computer products to customer order** has an overall business process BPD which is made up of collapsed sub-process. One of the sub-processes is called **Assemble components and test**. Contained in the expanded sub-process of **Assemble components and test** is a collapsed sub-process called **Test workstation**. The collapsed sub-processes below are expanded to show the three different levels of **granularity** i.e. high , medium and Low.

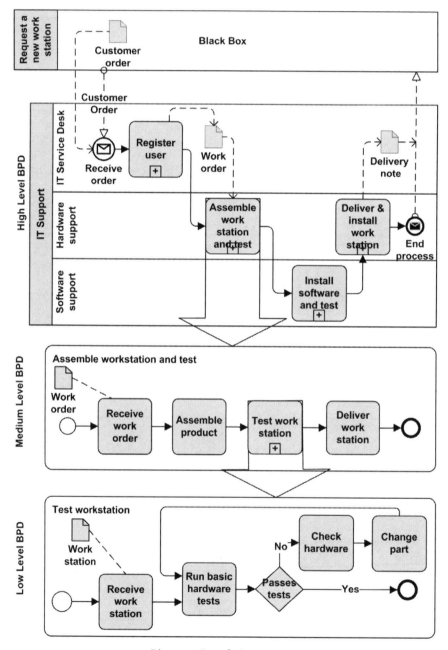

Diagram - Granularity process

Granularity considerations

The **Test workstation** is a low-level collapsed sub-process and describes the different tasks needed to fulfil the testing of the workstation before it leaves to be shipped. Most of these tasks would be difficult to **decompose** and make into a further sub-process level, although there could be such items as hardware or software test procedures which would have to be completed.

When decomposing collapsed sub-processes to a low level of **granularity**, it may be necessary to describe a specific task as a further collapsed sub-process. It would be possible to **decompose** parts of the low level collapsed sub-process, but the question is; is it a task, a procedure for doing something or actually a sub-process?

Instead of making too many levels of **granularity** it may be better to have more sub-processes in the high level BPD. This is always a trade-off, however in the end, the overall BPD must be easy to create, read, understand and maintain.

Notes

Call Activities

When modelling a business process, sometimes a task is needed which already exists in another process. In this case, it is better to include the existing task in the new process instead of modelling a new one. Using a *call activity* notation allows the modeller to reuse existing tasks already in operation and diminishes chances of creating inconsistencies. The modeller uses a *call activity* notation to represent calling a **global task** or **global process**.

A reusable element is considered a global task or process which could be an existing task such as credit check, (as this will be used as a standard task throughout the company and always uses the same procedure).

The activation of a *call activity* results in the transfer of control to the called global task or process. When the called activity is finished the control is transferred back to the original process.

A *call activity* notation shares the same shape as the task and sub-process notation. The *call activity* may have multi-instance and/or loop characteristic markers at the bottom centre of the shape, depending on the requirement. However, the type of activity will determine the details within the shape. The activity type can be unspecified, manual, user, business rule or script.

Call Activity Tasks

Unspecified Call Activity Notation

An *unspecified call activity* notation is shown by a thick lined rectangle with rounded corners.

Manual Call Activity Notation

A *manual call activity* notation is shown by a thick lined rectangle with rounded corners, containing a hand figure marker that distinguishes the shape as a manual task type.

User Call Activity Notation

A *user call activity* notation is shown by a thick lined rectangle with rounded corners, containing a human figure marker.

Business Rule Call Activity

A *business rule call activity* is shown by a thick lined rectangle with rounded corners, containing a chart shape in the upper left corner.

Script Call Activity Notation

A *script call activity* is shown by a thick lined rectangle with rounded corners, containing a script shape in the upper left corner.

Call Activity Sub-process

A Call Activity Calling a Process Notation

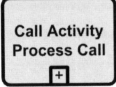

If details of a called process can be hidden, the shape of the *call activity calling a process* notation is shown by a thick lined rectangle with rounded corners, containing a plus sign.

Call Activity Calling a Process Expanded

The call activity can be expanded if the activity needs to be depicted.

Call Activity Calling a Process Expanded

If the details of the called process are available, then the shape of the *call activity calling a process expanded* will be the same as an expanded sub-process, drawn with a thick line

Exercise – call activities

The diagram below is the BDP of the sub-process **Receive order and confirm**, from the process of **Computer products to customer order**. Mark with a thick line which tasks could be termed **Global task** activities and what are their task types?

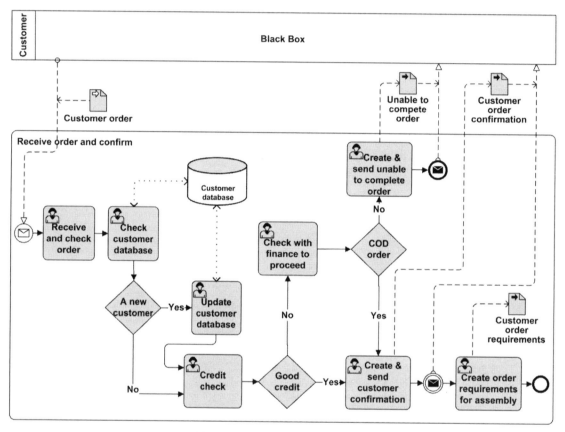

Diagram - Receive order and confirm

Boundary Intermediate Events

When an intermediate event notation is placed on the boundary (or edge) of an activity i.e. a task or a sub-process, it is a representation of how a business process responds to a deviation (exception) from the normal sequence flow of the process.

An exception flow is a sequence flow that originates from an *intermediate event* which is attached to the boundary of an activity. The process sequence will not deviate from this flow, unless an exception occurs during the performance of an activity (through an *intermediate boundary event*).

While intermediate events can be included in the normal flow to set delays or breaks to wait for a message, when they are attached to the boundary of an activity, a task or a sub-process, they create an exception flow.

Only the following types of intermediate events can be attached to the boundary of an activity

Message

Timer

Conditional

Parallel Multiple

Multiple

Signal

Any boundary intermediate event can be attached to any location of the activity boundary and the outgoing sequence flow can be drawn to flow in any direction. However, in the interest of clarity of the diagram, it is recommended that the modeller choose a consistent location on the boundary. Intermediate boundary events can be attached to the top or bottom of the activity and the sequence flow directed up or down. One or more intermediate events can be attached directly to the boundary of an activity. When attached to the boundary of an activity, the event can only "catch" the trigger.

Interrupt and Non-interrupt Boundary Intermediate Events

When a *boundary intermediate event* interrupts the sequence flow of a task or a sub-process the normal sequence flow stops, while the exception flow is completed. When the *boundary intermediate event* is non-interrupting, the normal sequence flow continues in parallel with the exception sequence flow.

Message Intermediate Boundary Event Notations

An interruptible *message intermediate boundary event* notation is depicted by two thin circles one drawn inside the other, containing an unfilled envelope.

A non-interruptible *message intermediate boundary event* notation is depicted by two thin dashed circles one drawn inside the other, containing an unfilled envelope.

The *message intermediate boundary event* notation is attached to the edge of a sub-process and when triggered changes the normal sequence flow into an exception sequence flow. When the *message intermediate boundary event* is non-interrupting, the normal sequence flow continues in parallel with the exception sequence flow. The actual participant, from which the message is received, is identified by connecting the sub-process to the participant using a message flow connector within a collaboration process.

A message event occurs when a message, with the exact identity as specified in the intermediate event, is received by the process. If this event does not occur when the event context is ready, then the process will continue through the normal flow as defined by the sequence flow.

Example of an Interruptible Message Intermediate Boundary Event

In this example, customers send orders which are handled by Handle orders sub-process. Each order will be processed and a work order produced. If a customer needs to cancel their order, the Handle Orders sub-process is interrupted and the exception path is followed to the Cancel work order task. After the order has been cancelled the sequence returns to the normal sequence flow to Update order records.

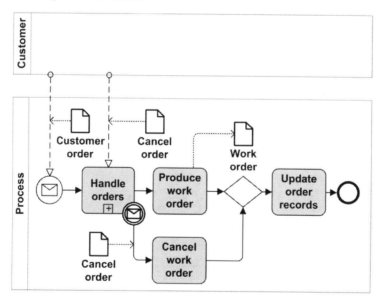

Diagram - Interruptible message intermediate boundary event

Question: Is it possible to have a *message intermediate boundary event* on a task?

Example of a Non-Interruptible Message Intermediate Boundary Event

When the *message intermediate boundary event* is non-interruptible, the Handle Orders sub-process continues while an order is updated.

In this example, customers send orders which are handled by Handle Orders sub-process. Each order will be processed and a work order produced. If a customer needs to change their order with a change order request, the Handle Orders sub-process will take an exception path to update the order. As the *message intermediate boundary event* is non-interruptible the normal sequence will continue.

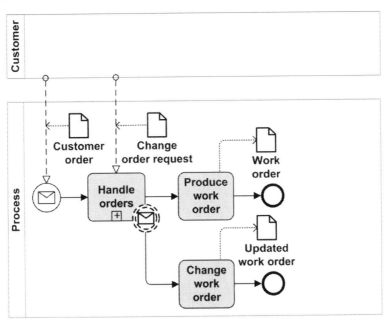

Diagram - Non-interruptible message intermediate boundary event

Question: Why is a non-interruptible message intermediate boundary event used in this diagram?

Timer Intermediate Boundary Event Notations

 An interruptible *timer intermediate boundary event* notation is depicted by two thin circles one drawn inside the other, containing a clock face.

 A non-interruptible *timer intermediate boundary event notation* is depicted with two thin dashed circles one drawn inside the other, containing a clock face.

The *timer intermediate boundary event* notation is placed on the edge of a task or sub-process in order to interrupt the sequence flow at a set time or date, during a task or sub-process activity. The set time or date causes the task or sub-process output to take an exception path.

Example of an Interruptible Timer Intermediate Boundary Event

In this example, daily invoices are checked and filed. If it is first day of the month, the normal sequence flow is interrupted, the exception flow takes precedence and the invoices are prepared and paid. The exception sequence flow returns to the normal sequence flow and invoices are filed.

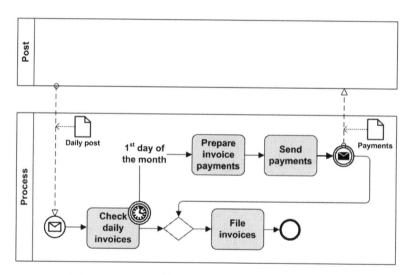

Diagram - Interruptible timer intermediate boundary event

Question: What happens if it is not the first day of the month?

Example of a Non-Interruptible Timer Intermediate Boundary Event

In this example, daily invoices are checked and filed. If it is first day of the month, the normal sequence flow is not interrupted and the exception flow is used in parallel. The exception flow prepares the invoice payments and payments are sent. The normal sequence flow continues filing the invoices.

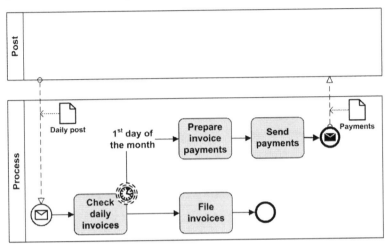

Diagram - Non-interruptible timer intermediate boundary event

Question: What is the use of a non-interruptible *timer intermediate boundary event* in this diagram?

Conditional Intermediate Boundary Event Notations

 An interruptible *conditional intermediate boundary event* notation is depicted by two thin circles one drawn inside the other, containing a rectangle with horizontal lines.

 A non-interruptible *conditional intermediate boundary event* notation is depicted by two thin dashed circles one drawn inside the other, containing a rectangle with horizontal lines.

The *conditional intermediate boundary event is used* as a business condition to change the normal flow into an exception flow.

Example of an Interruptible Conditional Intermediate Boundary Event

In this example, invoices are checked and filed. If payments are due, the normal sequence flow is interrupted and the payments are prepared and paid immediately. The exception flow returns to the normal sequence flow to file the invoices. When a specific business condition occurs, the sequence flow continues as an exception flow.

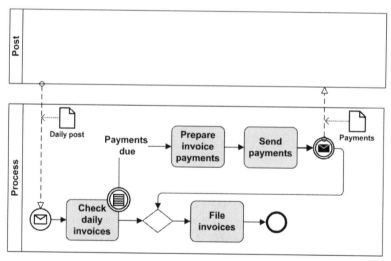

Diagram - Interruptible conditional intermediate boundary event

> Question: Could the diagram be modelled differently?

Example of a Non-Interruptible Conditional Intermediate Boundary Event

In this example, invoices are checked and filed. If payment is due, the normal sequence flow is not interrupted but the payments are prepared and paid immediately. The exception flow ends with payments being sent. As the normal sequence flow is not interrupted all invoices are filed.

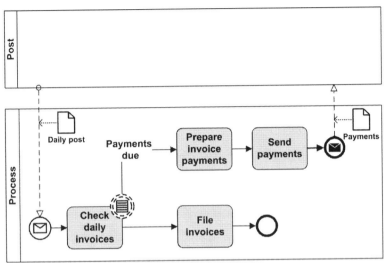

Diagram - Non-interruptible conditional intermediate boundary event

Parallel Multiple Intermediate Boundary Event Notations

 An interruptible *parallel multiple intermediate boundary event* notation is depicted by two thin circles one drawn inside the other, containing an unfilled plus sign.

 A non-interruptible *parallel multiple intermediate boundary e*vent notation is depicted by two thin dashed circles one drawn inside the other, containing an unfilled plus sign.

A *parallel multiple intermediate boundary event* is placed on the boundary of a task or sub-process. The exception flow is triggered when two or more different events occur simultaneously.

Example of an Interruptible Parallel Multiple Intermediate Boundary Event

In this example, invoices are checked and filed. If invoices are due **AND** it is the first day of the month, the normal sequence flow is interrupted and the payments are prepared and paid immediately. The exception flow returns to the normal sequence flow to file the invoices.

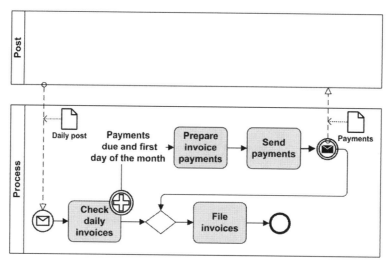

Diagram - Interruptible parallel multiple intermediate boundary event

Question: Which intermediate exception events have been replaced by the interruptible *parallel multiple intermediate boundary event* in the above diagram?

Example of a Non-Interruptible Parallel Multiple Intermediate Boundary Event

In this example, the invoices are checked and filed. If invoices are due **AND** it is the first day of the month, the normal sequence flow is not interrupted but payments are prepared and paid immediately, while the normal sequence flow files the invoices.

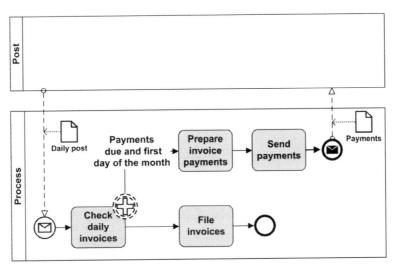

Diagram - Non-interruptible parallel multiple intermediate boundary event

Multiple Intermediate Boundary Event Notations

An interruptible *multiple intermediate boundary event* notation is depicted by two thin circles one drawn inside the other, containing an unfilled pentagon.

A non-interruptible *multiple intermediate boundary event* notation is depicted by two thin dashed circles one drawn inside the other, containing an unfilled pentagon.

The *multiple intermediate boundary event* is placed on the boundary of a task or sub-process to show that multiple intermediate events can trigger an exception flow. When used as an exception event and placed on the boundary of a task or sub-process, any of the designated events can trigger the exception flow. It is essential the event triggers are described on the diagram.

Example of an Interruptible Multiple Intermediate Boundary Event

In this example, invoices are checked and filed. If invoices are 30 days overdue **OR** the invoices are under a specific value, the normal sequence flow is interrupted and the payments are prepared and paid immediately. The exception flow returns to the normal sequence flow to file the invoices.

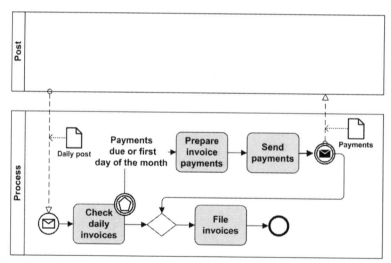

Diagram - Interruptible multiple intermediate boundary event

Question: What intermediate exception events are used in the above diagram?

Example of a Non-Interruptible Multiple Intermediate Boundary Event

In this example, invoices are checked and filed. If invoices are due **OR** it is the first day of the month, the normal sequence flow is interrupted payments are prepared and paid immediately. The normal sequence flow is not interrupted and the exception flow ends with payments sent while the normal sequence flow files the invoices.

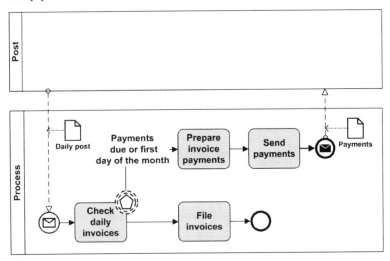

Diagram - Non-interruptible multiple intermediate boundary event

Choreography

Choreography defines the sequence of interactions between participants and only exists outside or in between process participant pools. A choreography sequence involves two or more participants and each sequence is made up of choreography activates and it is self-contained.

Choreography tasks and sub-processes consist of common BPMN elements, such as gateways and events. All the processes and their required interactions are depicted in a business process diagram. The status of the choreography is shown through the messages that are sent and received.

Choreography Tasks Elements

A choreography task is an activity in a choreography process. It represents an interaction, which is a set of message exchanges between two participants. Any communication between the participants is shown as a message flow.

A Choreography Task

A *choreography task* notation is a rectangle divided into three bands

The *initiating participant band* is used for the initiating participant name and is not shaded.

The *choreography task band* is in the centre of the notation and is used for the *choreography task name* and is not shaded.

The non-initiating participant band is used for the non-Initiating participant name and is shaded.

The *initiating participant band* can be either at the top or at the bottom. The *non-initiating participant band* can be either at the bottom or at the top.

Unspecified/None Choreography Task Notation

The *unspecified/none choreography task* notation is a rectangle divided into three bands without distinguishing markers.

Choreography Task – Loop Notation

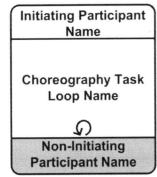

A *choreography task -loop* notation is divided into three bands. The choreography task name band contains an arrow loop symbol positioned at the centre bottom.

Choreography Task - Sequential Multi Instance Notation

```
┌─────────────────────────┐
│  Initiating Participant  │
│          Name            │
├─────────────────────────┤
│                         │
│    Choreography Task    │
│     Sequential Multi    │
│      Instance Name      │
│                         │
│           ≡             │
├─────────────────────────┤
│     Non-Initiating      │
│    Participant Name     │
└─────────────────────────┘
```

A *choreography task - sequential multi instance* notation is divided into three bands. The choreography task band contains three parallel horizontal lines at centre bottom.

Choreography Task - Parallel Multi Instance Notation

```
┌─────────────────────────┐
│  Initiating Participant  │
│          Name            │
├─────────────────────────┤
│                         │
│    Choreography Task    │
│  Parallel Multi Instance │
│          Name           │
│                         │
│           |||           │
├─────────────────────────┤
│     Non-Initiating      │
│    Participant Name     │
└─────────────────────────┘
```

A *choreography task - parallel multi instance* notation is divided into three bands. The choreography task band contains three parallel vertical lines at centre bottom.

Choreography Sequence Flow

Sequence flows are used with choreographies to show the sequence of the choreography activities, which may also have intervening gateways to show forks, mergers and events. Sequence flows cannot cross the boundary of a *sub-choreography* and are only allowed to connect to other choreography activities.

Example of Messages with a Choreography Task

In this example, the choreography task is part of a collaboration process. The message flows will pass through a choreography task as they connect from one participant to another i.e. customer and supplier. The buyer (customer pool) sends an order to the seller (supplier pool) with an *initiating message*. The seller confirms the order depicted by a *non-initiating message*.

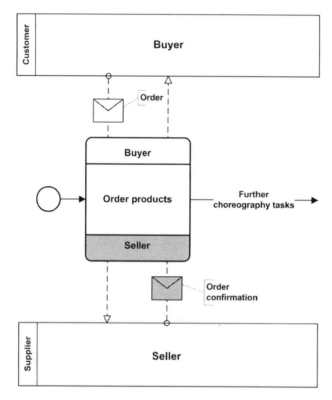

Diagram - Messages with a choreography task

A Sub-Choreography – Collapsed Unspecified/ None Notation

A *sub-choreography – collapsed* unspecified/none *notation* is a rectangle divided into three bands. The *sub-choreography - collapsed name* contains a plus sign within a box at bottom centre.

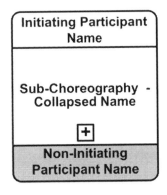

The *sub-choreography – collapsed band* is in the centre of the notation and used for the *sub-choreography – collapsed name* and is not shaded.

The details of the *sub-choreography - collapsed* are not visible in the diagram but the symbol indicates that the activity is a sub-process and has a lower level of detail.

Sub-Choreography Loop - Collapsed Notation

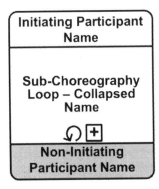

A *sub-choreography loop – collapsed notation* is divided into three bands. The *sub-choreography loop – collapsed name band* contains a loop symbol, next to a plus sign within a box at centre bottom.

Sub-Choreography Sequential Multi-Instance – Collapsed Notation

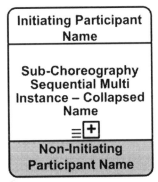

A sub-choreography sequential multi instance - collapsed notation is divided into three bands. The choreography sequential multi instance - *collapsed name* band contains the sequential multi-instance symbol, three horizontal lines, next to a plus sign within a box at centre bottom.

Sub-Choreography Parallel Multi Instance - Collapsed Notation

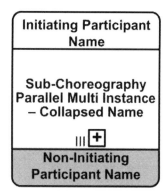

A *sub-choreography parallel multi instance - collapsed* notation is divided into three bands. The sub-choreography *parallel multi instance - collapsed name* band contains the parallel multi-instance symbol, three vertical lines, next to a plus sign within a box at centre bottom.

Example of Two Choreography Tasks

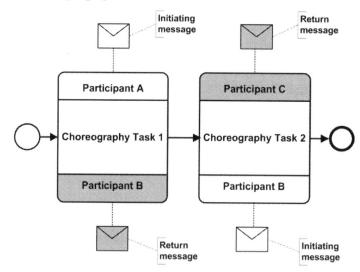

Diagram – Two choreography tasks

The above diagram shows a sequence of two choreography tasks with three participants.

1. Participant A sends a message and is the initiator of choreography Task 1.

2. Participant B responds with a message, which may not be immediate, since there can be internal work that participant B needs to fulfil, prior to sending the return message.

3. Participant B sends a new message and is the initiator of choreography Task 2.

4. Participant C does not know exactly when the message will arrive from participant B, but is aware that one will arrive.

Example of Choreography Task Sequence

The following diagram shows a sequence of four choreography tasks with two participants **i.e.** Customer and Company.

1. Customer sends an order via email to Company

2. Company responds with a confirmation email

3. The product is delivered

4. Company sends an invoice

5. Customer sends a cheque

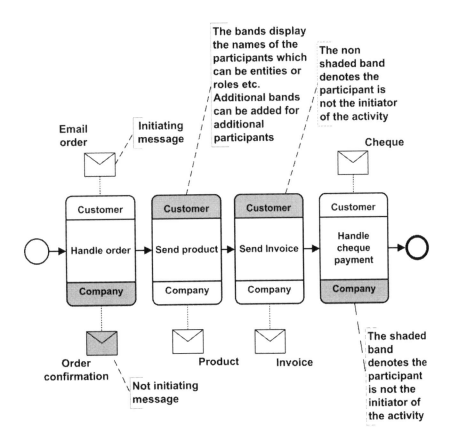

Diagram - Choreography task sequence

Question: Could other messages be included in the above diagram?

Example of a Choreography within a Collaboration Process

1. The customer sends an order via email to Computer Product Supplier.
2. The Computer Product Supplier responds with a confirmation email.
3. The sequence ends with Computer Product Supplier sending an invoice.

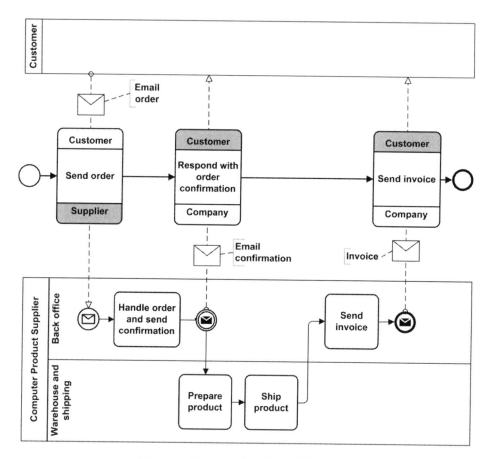

Diagram – Choreography within collaboration

Exercise - choreography within collaboration

List other message exchanges which could be included in the above diagram

-

-

-

Signal Events

Signal Events are used for general communication within and across process levels, pools and between BPD's.

Signal Start Event Notations

 A *signal start event* notation is depicted by a circle, containing an unfilled triangle.

 A *signal start event* notation used as a non-*interrupt event* is depicted by a dashed line circle, containing an unfilled triangle.

This type of event is used for sending or receiving signals. The *signal start interrupt event* is used to start a top level process sequence or to start a sub-process. A signal arrives that has been broadcast from another process and triggers the start.

Note that the signal is not a message. A message has a specific target.

The *signal start non-interrupt event is only used* to start a sub-process.

A *signal start event* is triggered by a signal throwing event from another process, which is either an *end signal event* or an *intermediates signal throwing event*, broadcasting a signal from another process.

Example of a Signal Start Event

In the following example, the task *Check customer orders* will only start when a signal is received from another process.

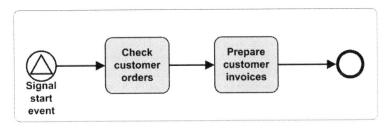

Diagram – Signal start event

Signal Intermediate Events

This type of intermediate event can send or receive a signal if the event is part of a normal flow. When used to "catch" the signal, the event marker is unfilled. When used to "throw" the signal, the event marker is filled.

Signal Intermediate Catching Event Notation

 A *signal intermediate catching event notation is depicted by* two circles one drawn inside the other, containing an unfilled triangle.

The *signal intermediate catching event* is used to receive signals in the same way as a *signal start event*. The *signal intermediate catching event* waits until a trigger arrives from a *signal end event* or a *signal intermediate throwing event,* before starting the process sequence.

Signal Intermediate Throwing Event Notation

 A *signal intermediate throwing event notation is depicted by* two circles one drawn inside the other, containing a filled triangle.

The *signal intermediate throwing event* is used to send a signal while in an inline process, to either a *signal start event* or a *signal intermediate catching event.*

Example of a Signal Intermediate Event

In the following example, the monthly invoices are prepared and sent to accounting. When the accounting is updated and invoices are filed, payments are sent. Accounting checks all payable invoices but the invoice handling process must wait for the *signal intermediate catching event,* to be triggered. Once accounting is satisfied with the invoices they will proceed to update the accounts and at the same time, trigger the *signal intermediate throwing event,* which starts the payment process.

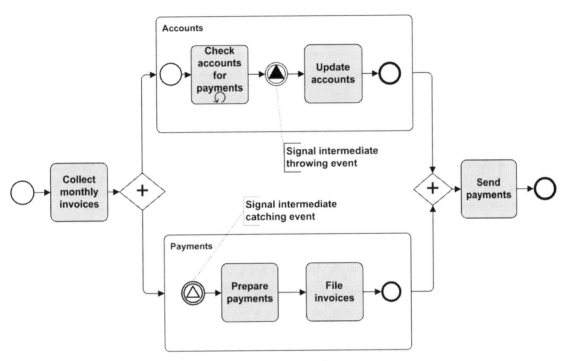

Diagram - Signal intermediate events

Question: What gateways are used in the above diagram?

Signal End Event Notation

 A *signal end event* notation is depicted by a circle containing a filled triangle.

The *signal end event* is a throwing event and indicates that a signal will be broadcast to either a signal start or signal intermediate catching event in another process. Note that the *signal end event* is not a message event (which has a specific source and target).

Example of a Signal End Event

The customer's order is received and credit checked. If the customer is creditworthy, the product is shipped, customer records are updated and a work order produced. The sequence flow ends with a *signal end event* which triggers the sub-process *Despatch product*, which is waiting start with a *signal start event*. If the customer is not creditworthy, the exception sequence is taken and an order cancellation is produced and sent to the customer.

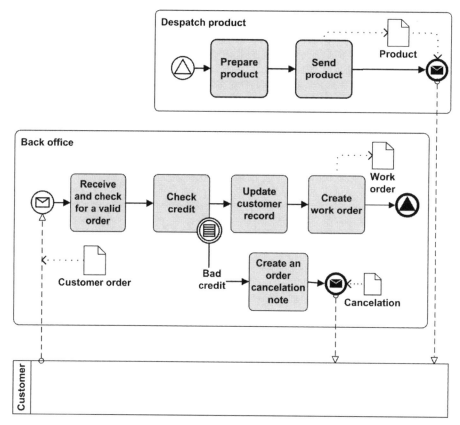

Diagram - Signal end event

Question: In the above diagram what is the boundary event and what triggers it?

Signal Intermediate Boundary Event Notations

 An *signal intermediate boundary event* notation is depicted by two thin circles one drawn inside the other, containing an unfilled triangle.

 A *signal intermediate boundary event* notation used as a non-*interrupt event* is *depicted by* two thin dashed circles one drawn inside the other, containing an unfilled triangle.

The *signal intermediate boundary event* is a catching event attached to the edge of an activity and is triggered by a *task exception. The signal intermediate boundary event* diverts the sequence flow taking the exception sequence flow.

If the *signal intermediate boundary event* is an interrupt event, the normal sequence flow ceases and the exception path is followed. If the *signal intermediate boundary event* is a non-interrupt event, the normal sequence flow continues at the same time as the exception sequence flow. The *signal intermediate boundary event triggers any signal start event or signal intermediate event.*

Example of a Signal Intermediate Boundary Event

In the following example, the monthly invoices are prepared and sent to accounting and the invoice handling departments. Accounting will check the accounts of each invoice. The invoice handling will prepares each invoice. If an invoice is to be paid, the signal intermediate boundary event will trigger the signal intermediate catching event, activating the *Prepare payments* task.

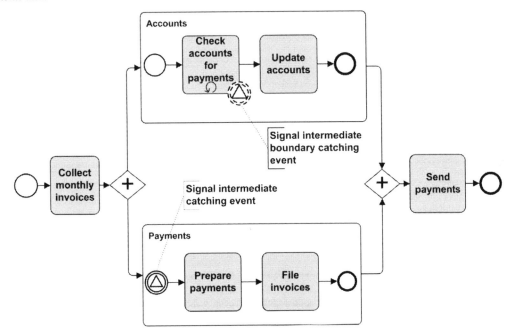

Diagram - Signal intermediate boundary event

Error and Cancel Events

Error Events

There are three types of error events, a start event, an intermediate boundary event and an end event. An error event can only be used to interrupt a process.

Error Start Event Notation

An *error start event* notation is depicted by a circle containing an unfilled lightning marker.

The *error start event* is used as an in-line event sub-process and will always interrupt the sequence flow.

Example of an Error Handler Sub-process

The error handler is triggered by an *error start event* from an *error end event* in another sub-process.

The customer's order records are checked and a cancelation order is prepared and sent to the customer.

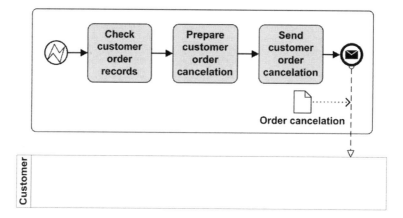

Diagram - Error handler

Error Intermediate Boundary Event Notation

 An error intermediate boundary event notation is depicted by two circles one drawn inside the other, containing an unfilled lightning marker.

The *error intermediate boundary event* notation is attached to the edge of a task or sub-process to catch a specific or an unspecified error. An *error intermediate boundary event* triggers an error handler. This type of event can only be attached to the boundary of an activity or sub-process. The process may define an additional error handling sub-process.

Error End Event Notation

 An error end event *notation* is depicted by a thick circle containing a filled lightning marker.

The *error end event* is a throwing event and generates an error condition which is used to stop a process sequence. The error condition is caught by an *error intermediate boundary event* which is situated on the edge of a sub-process. The behaviour of the process is unspecified if an *error intermediate boundary event* is not used.

Example of Error End Events and Intermediate Boundary Events

The customer's order is received and credit checked. If the customer is creditworthy, the product is shipped. If the customer is not creditworthy the sequence flow ends with an *error end event*. The *error end event* triggers the *error intermediate boundary event,* which is attached to the edge of the sub-process, which in turn triggers the *Handle bad credit* sub-process.

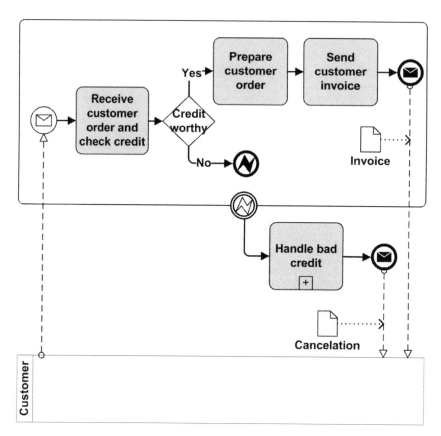

Diagram - Error end events and intermediate boundary events

Cancel Events

The cancel events are always used as a pair. An *error intermediate boundary event* is triggered by a *cancel end event*.

Cancel End Event Notation

A *cancel end event* notation is depicted by a thick circle containing a solid **X**.

The *cancel end event* indicates that all activities in the process sequence cease immediately without compensation, including multi-Instances. The *cancel end event* is a throwing event and therefore the behaviour of the process is unspecified if a *cancel intermediate boundary event* is not present. This type of end event is used within a sub-process and indicates that the activity is cancelled.

Cancel Intermediate Boundary Event Notation

A *cancel intermediate boundary event* notation is depicted by two circles containing an unfilled **X**.

The *cancel intermediate boundary event* notation is used only on the boundary of a sub-process. The *cancel intermediate boundary event* is a catching event, triggered only by the cancel end event within the sub-process.

When using a *cancel end event* in the process sequence, it is advisable to use a cancel handler sub-process. The *cancel end event* stops the sequence flow and does not react to any other activity. Using a *cancel intermediate event* allows the modeller to create an activity which handles the condition of a cancel situation. According to the BPMN specification, the *cancel end event* throws a trigger to a capture *cancel intermediate event*, which is situated on a boundary of a sub-process. The *cancel intermediate event* continues the sequence flow to a cancel event handler sub-process.

Example of Cancel Events

In the following example, orders are received from a customer. The credit is checked and if the customer is creditworthy, the product is shipped. If the customer is not creditworthy, the customer records are updated and the sequence finishes with a *cancel end event*. The *cancel end event* is captured by a *cancel intermediate boundary event*, directing the sequence flow to the sub-process, Handle order cancelation.

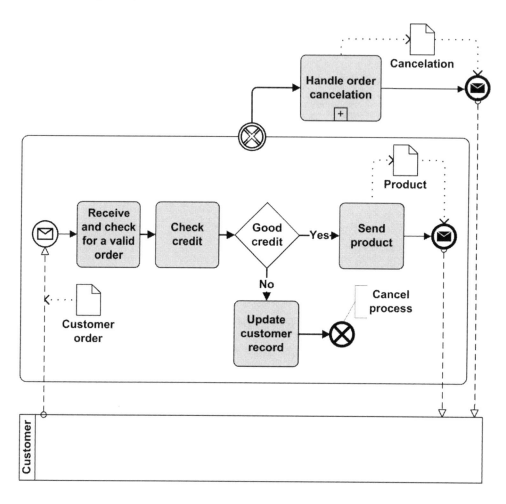

Diagram - Cancel events

Question: Why does the Handle order cancelation sub-process stop with a message end event?

Escalation Events

Escalation Start Event Notation

An interrupt *escalation start event* notation is depicted by a circle, containing an upturned, unfilled arrowhead.

A non-interrupt *escalation start event* notation is depicted by a dashed circle, containing an upturned, unfilled arrowhead.

The *escalation start event* cannot be used as a top level event and is only used to trigger an in-line event sub-process. The *escalation start event* can be used as an interrupt or as a non-interrupt event in an inline sub-process, depending on the process requirements.

Escalation Intermediate Boundary Event Notation

An *escalation intermediate interrupt boundary event* notation is depicted by two thin circles one drawn inside the other, containing an unfilled, upturned arrowhead.

An *escalation intermediate non-interrupt boundary event* notation is depicted by two thin circles with dashed lines one drawn inside the other, containing an unfilled, upturned arrowhead.

The *escalation intermediate boundary event* notation can only be attached to the boundary of a task or sub-process. The outgoing sequence flow or exception sequence flow is used in association with an escalation handler. The *escalation intermediate boundary event* can either be used as an interrupt or as a non-interrupt event in an inline sub-process, depending on the process requirements.

Escalation Intermediate Throwing Event Notation

An *escalation intermediate throwing event* notation is depicted by two thin circles one drawn inside the other, containing an upturned, filled arrowhead.

The *escalation intermediate throwing event* is an event which is caught by an *escalation intermediate boundary event* on the edge of a sub-process.

The behaviour of the *escalation intermediate throwing event* is unspecified if it is not associated with an *escalation intermediate boundary event*.

Escalation End Event Notation

An *escalation end event* notation is depicted by a circle drawn with a thick solid line, containing a filled, upturned arrowhead.

The *escalation end event* is a throwing event which is caught by an *escalation intermediate boundary event* on the edge of a sub-process. The behaviour of the *escalation end event* is unspecified if it is not associated with an *escalation intermediate boundary event*.

Example of Escalation Events

In the following example, a customer order is received and credit is checked. If the customer's credit is approved, the product is shipped and the sequence flow ends with a message end event.

If the customer is not credit worthy, the customer records are updated and the escalation intermediate throwing event triggers the *escalation intermediate non-interrupting boundary event,* which in turn triggers the Cancel order handler sub-process. The sub-process ends, after the Remove order task, with an unspecified end event

The Cancel order handler prepares and sends a cancelation with message end event.

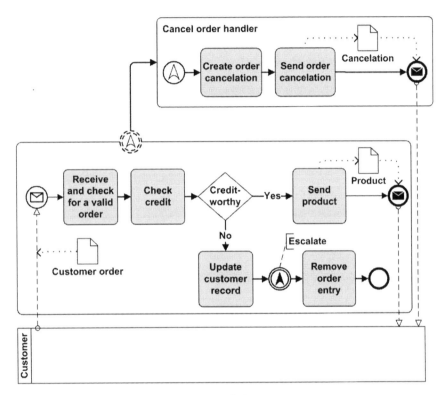

Diagram - Escalation events

Compensation Events

Compensation is about undoing steps that were already successfully completed. Compensation events undo what has already been done, in reverse order. Note that interrupting a non-interrupting aspect of other events does not apply in the case of a *compensation event*.

An activity that might require compensation is one that charges a buyer for a service and debits a credit card, however the service cannot be provided, therefore the credit card needs to be backed out. Often, a record of both activities is required which is another reason why the first activity is not "undone."

General Notes on Compensation

Only activities that are completed can be compensated.

The compensation of an activity can be triggered in two ways

1. The activity is inside a transaction sub-process that is cancelled. In this situation, the whole sub-process is "rewound" or rolled back, the process flow goes backwards and any activity that requires compensation is compensated. This is why the compensation marker for events looks like a "rewind" symbol for a tape player. After the compensation has been completed, the process continues its rollback.

2. A compensation intermediate or compensation end event, "throws" a compensation identifier that is "caught" by the intermediate event attached to the boundary of the activity.

The compensation is thrown in two ways

1. The event specifically identifies an activity that requires compensation.

2. The event broadcasts the need for the compensation, then all completed activities that have a *compensation intermediate catching event* attached (associated) to their boundaries are compensated. The compensation applies to all activities that have been fully completed within the process (which includes all levels of the process). The compensation occurs in the reverse order of the original performance on the triggered activities.

Compensation Task and Sub-process Notations

The *task* and *collapsed sub-process* notations are graphically shown by the same rounded corner rectangular symbol however, the *collapsed sub-process* has a plus sign centre bottom.

The *compensation* notation is represented by a small symbol that looks like the rewind-button on an tape player i.e. two small solid triangles pointing left. The compensation task or *collapsed sub-process* is only required when a specified task or sub-process needs to be undone (unwound).

Compensation Start Event Notation

A *compensation start event* notation is depicted by a circle drawn with a thin line, containing an unfilled double triangle marker pointing left.

The *compensation start event* is only used to start an in-line compensation event sub-process. The process compensation takes place after the process has been completed and can only be triggered by the completion of the process.

Example of a Compensation Handler

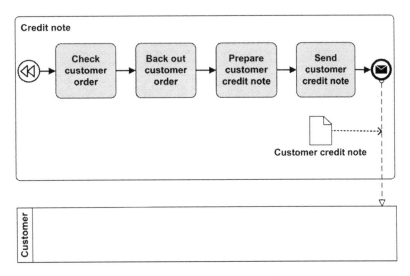

Diagram - Compensation handler

Compensation Intermediate Boundary Event Notation

 A *compensation intermediate boundary event* notation is depicted by two thin circles one drawn inside the other, containing an unfilled double triangle marker pointing left.

The *compensation intermediate boundary event* notation is attached to the edge of a task or sub-process indicating that compensation is necessary for that activity. When a *compensation intermediate boundary event* is attached to the edge of an activity, the event is triggered by a throwing compensation event which identifies that activity or a broadcast compensation.

If the event identifies an activity, then that activity (and no other) will be compensated. Otherwise, the compensation is broadcast to all activities that have been completed within the process.

Note that there is only one target activity for compensation. There cannot be a sequence of activities. If the compensation requires more than one activity, then these activities must be put inside a single sub-process that is the target of the association. The sub-process can be collapsed or expanded. If the sub-process is expanded, only the sub-process itself requires the compensation marker. The activities inside the sub-process do not require this marker.

Example of Compensation Activity

This example shows the compensation association of an activity. If monthly accounting creates an invoice for a customer and their product has been returned a credit note will be generated for the customer. This compensation activity cannot take place until the sequence finds a *compensation intermediate throwing event* or a *compensation end event*.

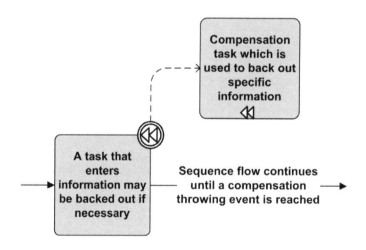

Diagram - Compensation activity

The sequence flow from a task to a compensation task is shown by a dashed line. Compensation takes place after a compensation throwing event is reached.

Compensation Intermediate Throwing Event Notation

A *compensation intermediate throwing event* notation is depicted by two thin circles, containing a filled double triangle marker pointing left.

The *compensation intermediate throwing event* is used in a normal sequence flow and indicates that if any compensation is necessary, the compensation is executed at that time. If the *compensation intermediate throwing event* identifies an activity, then the activity which will be compensated. The *compensation intermediate throwing event* broadcasts to all activities which have been completed within the process, including the top-level process and all sub-processes. In order to be compensated, a task or sub-process must have a compensation intermediate boundary event notation attached to it.

Compensation End Event Notation

A *compensation end event notation* is depicted by a circle drawn with a thick line, containing a filled double triangle marker pointing left.

The *compensation* end event is an event which triggers the processing of all *compensation intermediate boundary events* in the process. If an activity is identified in the process sequence flow which needs compensating, it is compensated. The compensation *end event* allows tasks or sub-processes to be "undone" using a specific compensation task or sub-process.

Example of Compensation Intermediate and End Events

In the following example, the monthly invoices are prepared and returned products are checked. The *compensation intermediate throwing event* is an inline event and instigates compensation when necessary. If products have been returned, invoices are nullified for these customers and not sent. The task *Nullify invoices and update customer records* is a compensation task and prevents the customer receiving an invoice for a product which has been returned.

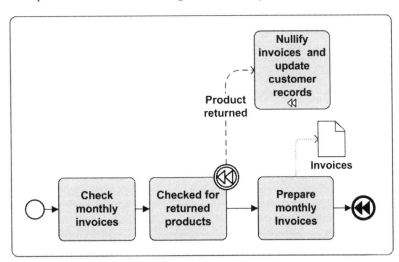

Diagram - Compensation intermediate and end events

Example of Compensation Intermediate Boundary and Throwing Events

In the following example, the monthly invoices are prepared and returned products are checked. If products have been returned, the compensation intermediate throwing event will trigger the compensation intermediate boundary event to start the compensation. Where customers have returned products the compensation task will nullify the invoices. The sub-process ends with a message end event.

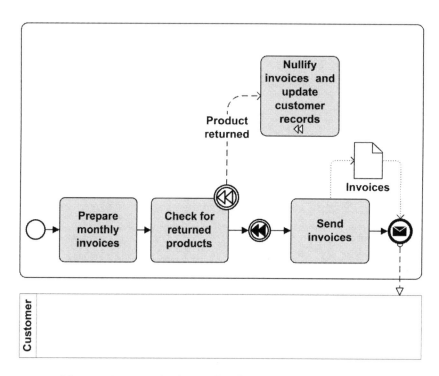

Diagram - Compensation intermediate boundary and throwing events

Note that unless an activity has been identified, all activities that are completed within the process, starting with the top-level process and all sub-processes, are subject to compensation proceeding in reverse order.

Collapsed Event Sub-Process

A collapsed event sub-process is a specialised sub-process and not part of the normal sequence flow of its parent process,. There is no incoming or outgoing sequence flow, it is a standalone sub-process. It may or may not occur while the parent process is active, however, if the parent process is active, it is possible that it will occur many times. Collapsed event sub-processes are self-contained and are not connected to the rest of the sequence flow.

Unlike a standard sub-process, which uses the flow of the parent process as a trigger, a collapsed event sub-process has only one start event with a trigger. Each time the start event is triggered while the parent process is active, the collapsed event sub-process will commence. Collapsed event sub-processes cannot have attached boundary events.

There are two possible consequences to the parent process when an *event sub-process* is triggered:

1. the parent process can be interrupted
2. the parent process can continue and not be interrupted

This is determined by the type of start event used.

More than one non-interrupting *collapsed event sub-process* can be initiated at different times.

A *collapsed event sub-process* has the option to retrigger the event through which it was triggered, to allow the continuation outside the boundary of the associated sub-process. Event sub-processes have a start event with a trigger notation of one of the following:

Message, Timer, Conditional, Multiple, Parallel Multiple, Escalation, Signal, Error and Compensation

Collapsed Event Sub-process Notations

All *collapsed event sub-process* notations are depicted as a dotted line rectangle, containing a plus sign bottom centre and share the same basic shape as the sub-process object.

Message Event Sub-Process Notations

The *message event sub-process interrupting trigger* notation is a thin solid line circle with a non filled envelope. The non-interrupting trigger notation is a thin dotted circle containing a non filled envelope. *Message event sub-processes* are triggered by a message with the same behaviour as the receive task.

Timer Event Sub-Process Notations

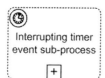

The *timer event sub-process interrupting trigger* notation is a thin solid line circle, containing a clock face. The non-interrupting trigger notation is a thin dotted circle containing a clock face. *Timer event sub-processes are* triggered by a specific date and time.

Conditional Event Sub-Process Notations

The *conditional event sub-process interrupting trigger* notation is a thin solid line circle, containing a rectangle with three horizontal lines. The non-interrupting trigger notation is a thin dotted circle, containing a rectangle with three horizontal lines. *Conditional event sub-processes are* triggered by a specific condition occurring.

Multiple Event Sub-Process Notations

 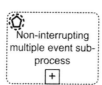

The *multiple event sub-process interrupting trigger* notation is a thin solid line circle, containing a pentagon. The non-interrupting trigger notation is a thin dotted circle, containing a pentagon. *Multiple event sub-processes are* triggered by receiving any combination of a message event, a timer event, a conditional event or a signal event.

Parallel Multiple Event Sub-Process Notations

 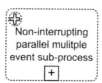

The *parallel multiple event sub-process interrupting trigger* notation is a thin solid line circle, containing a non-filled plus sign. The non-interrupting trigger notation is a thin dotted circle, containing a non-filled plus sign. *Multiple event sub-processes are* triggered by receiving any combination of a message event, a timer event, a conditional event or a signal event occurring at the same time.

Escalation Event Sub-Process Notations

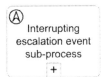 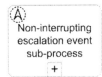

The *escalation event sub-process interrupting trigger* notation is a thin solid line circle, containing an upturned solid line arrowhead. The non-interrupting trigger notation is a thin dotted circle, containing an upturned solid line arrowhead. *Escalation event sub-processes are* triggered by an escalation throwing event.

Signal Event Sub-Process Notations

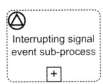 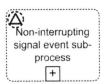

The *signal event sub-process interrupting trigger* notation is a thin solid line circle, containing a triangle. The non-interrupting trigger notation is a thin dotted circle, containing a triangle. *Signal event sub-processes are* triggered by a throwing signal event from another process.

Error Event Sub-Process

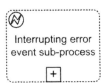

The *error event sub-process interrupting trigger* notation is drawn with a thin solid line circle, containing an unfilled lightning marker. *Error event sub-processes* are triggered by a throwing error event from another process notation and are only an interrupting trigger.

Compensation Event Sub-Process

The *compensation event sub-process interrupting trigger* notation is drawn with a thin solid line circle, containing an unfilled double triangle. *Compensation event sub-process* are triggered by a throwing compensation event and are only an interrupting trigger

Modelling a Procurement Process

This is an example of a procurement process which is used by a procurement department

This process is broken into four sub-processes:

1. Prepare requirements and select procedure
2. Select suppliers based on business rules
3. Registration of tenders and select supplier
4. Review financial commitments and order

The following diagram shows the overview procurement process sequence of sub-processes. Every time an employee requests products or services from a supplier the following procurement process is followed.

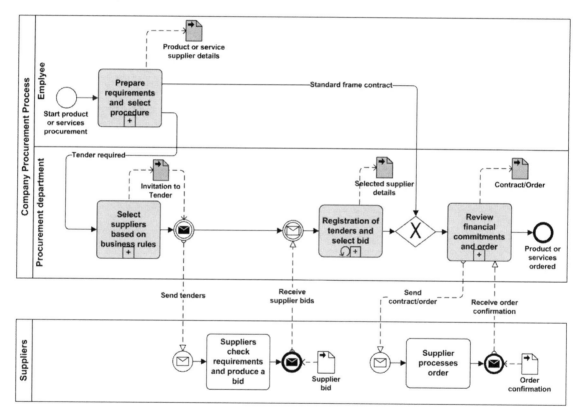

Diagram - Overview procurement process

Procurement business rules

Rule	Purchasing thresholds	Offers Required
1	€ 0 to € 500	Not required
2	€ 0 to € 5,000	Minimum of one vendor for products or services to be supplied (fax, copy catalogue, email or copy website are acceptable as an offer).
3	€ 5,000 to € 25,000	Send a Request to Tender to a minimum 3 vendors
4	€ 25,000 to € 60,000	Send Request to Tender to a minimum 5 vendors

Prepare requirements and select procedure

The following diagram is the sub-process to prepare the procurement requirements and select the procedure. The procurement process has different business rules depending on the contract situation. If the procurement department already has a framework contract for a specific supplier, there is no need to go to tender. Otherwise the requirement would be to go to tender for the product or service.

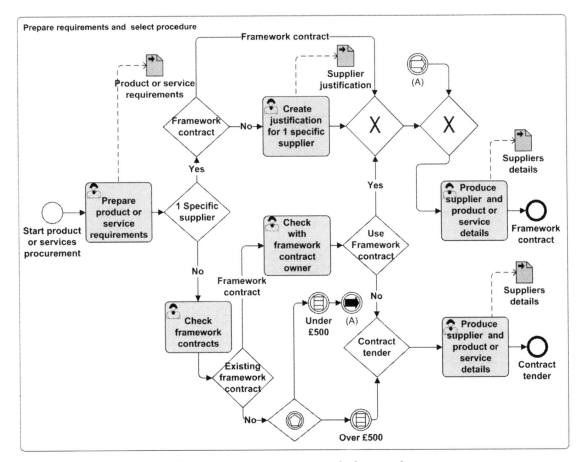

Diagram - Prepare requirements and select procedure

Select number of suppliers based on business rules

The following diagram is the sub-process to select suppliers based on business rules. The business rules will vary but for this example, the conditions are under £5000, under £25000 and over £60000.

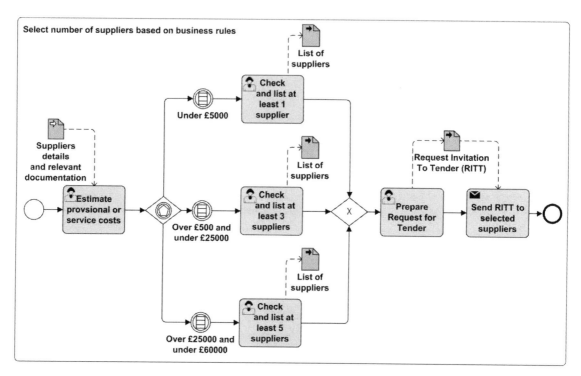

Diagram - Select number of suppliers based on business rules

Registration of tenders and select supplier

The following diagram is the sub-process for the registration of tenders and supplier selection. The tender selection procedure has to be in place with predetermined criteria. The tenders received are stored until a predetermined date, before opening.

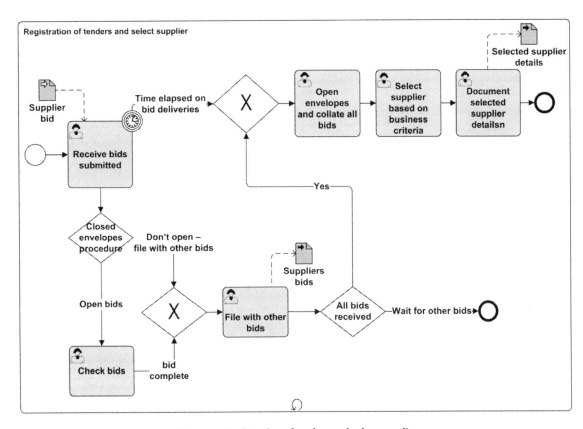

Diagram - Registration of tenders and select supplier

Question: Why is the above BPD a looping sub-process and what triggers the end of the looping?

Review financial commitments and order

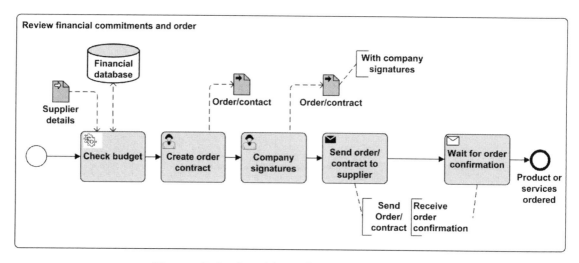

Diagram - Review financial commitments and order

Exercise – list business rules

List all the business rules for this process?

-
-
-
-
-
-
-
-
-
-

Further Reading

Kenneth Sherry is also the author of '**Insight Into Business Processes**'. The book gives a clear and comprehensive overview of business processes for those who are seeking an insight in today's modern business process management.

The following is an overview of some of the topics covered in 'Insight Into Business Processes'.

- Business process management
- Business process modelling
- Business rules
- Gathering business process requirements
- Business process documentation
- Business process fulfilment staff procedures
- The role of the business process analyst

29405969R00077

Printed in Great Britain
by Amazon